Get the
PICTURE YOU WANT
ESSENTIAL DIGITAL PHOTOGRAPHY TECHNIQUES

by the Element K Journals Creative Team

**Peachpit
Press**

Get the Picture You Want
Essential Digital Photography Techniques
The Element K Journals Creative Team

Peachpit Press

1249 Eighth Street
Berkeley, CA 94710
510/524-2178
800/283-9444
510/524-2221 (fax)

Find us on the World Wide Web at:
www.peachpit.com

To report errors, please send a note to
errata@peachpit.com

Peachpit Press is a division of Pearson Education.

Published in association with Element K Journals.

Copyright © 2005 by Element K Journals

Production Team

Editor: Stephen Dow

Contributing Editors: G.H. Cloutier, Renée Dustman, Toby Mikle, Amy Palermo, Jim Whitcomb, Ron Wilder, Paul Wood

Project Editor: Jan Mater-Cavagnaro

Production Editor: Lisa Brazieal

Copy Editors: Leesa Israel and Christine Hunt

Cover and Interior Design: Alicia Natale

Senior Vice President and Publisher: Doreen Bieryla

Associate Publisher: Michelle Rogers

Graphic Design Manager: Charles Willey

ISBN 0-321-30338-5

9 8 7 6 5 4 3 2 1
Printed and bound in the United States of America

Get the
PICTURE YOU WANT

To the big fish,
for believing that her little fish
could swim in a bigger pond.

TABLE OF CONTENTS

Part 1—Getting Started

It's pretty safe to say that digital photography has become the darling of consumer technology over the past few years. With the improvement in quality and the decrease in price, digital cameras have certainly hit the sweet spot for the creative consumer.

In this part, we'll introduce you to the wonders of digital photography, show you how the cameras work, and explain what all the fuss is about. We'll also show you how to extend the life of your camera and lenses and how to get your money's worth from your batteries by taking care of your investment. Along the way, we'll give you tips on getting the most from your digital camera.

Why go digital?

Ever since its exponential growth in the late '90s, digital photography has become a more integral part of the photographic world. Whether you're a professional photographer using digital cameras for high-end photo shoots, a hardcore enthusiast capturing your family events and vacations, or a professional who uses digital shots for company business, the use of digital photography has likely become an important and regular component to your routine.

I want it now!

Versatility and instant gratification are the two key reasons digital photography has grown at such a blinding rate. Digital cameras blend the ease of use and features of a quality 35 mm camera with the instant gratification of a Polaroid®. With a digital camera, you can go from capturing an image to looking at the high-quality printout in just a few minutes. You can take a picture, download it to your computer, and have it instantly emailed to all of your friends. Or you can take a photo of an important new item and have it posted to the Web for the world to see within a matter of a few seconds. That speed would never be possible using a conventional film camera.

A picture for later

Duplication is also a key feature of digital photography. In the film world, the only way you can get good duplicates is by reprinting the photo from the negative—and that assumes that the negative isn't damaged. If a negative is scratched or shows signs of aging, the resulting print may be less than perfect.

In the digital world, the picture file is comprised of a series of zeros and ones, with special additional information to make sure that the file isn't corrupted. Because of this, a digital picture never changes. The first print will look as vibrant and detailed as the millionth print.

Storage and archiving

Since film media is sensitive, you need to carefully store the negatives if you want them to be available for later use. Protecting the negatives requires special non-reactive sleeves to hold the negatives and a climate-controlled area to store them. Unfortunately, even the best care can't ensure the negative will survive a couple of centuries from now.

Film photography can also be difficult to archive. Sure, you can write down the subject and date of the photos on the negative sleeve, but locating a particular photo can still take hours. Due to the nature of the media, it isn't possible to duplicate a film archive in two locations, both for security and convenience. Though you could conceivably duplicate the negatives, you'd lose image quality as well as money in the long run.

Storing and archiving digital photos, however, is a snap. You can download the images to a disk and then burn duplicate copies to any number of CDs or DVDs without losing a bit of quality. And you can import the photos into any number of archiving applications that will help you sort and store the images. These same applications also make it easy to locate a single photo from the entire library with ease.

The power of competition

Competition is the driving force behind the rapid advancement of digital photography. From traditional film companies, such as Kodak and Nikon, to more electronics-based companies, like Sony and Canon, the chance to get in on the ground floor of this emerging technology has led to constant innovation and improvement of digital-based equipment and related software. Consumer-level cameras in the 5 MP range were unheard of two years ago but are commonplace today. In fact, in the professional area, some high-end camera manufacturers are testing digital cameras that operate in the 20 MP range, taking the digital image close

to and beyond the detail of the best film. Improvements in memory systems, CCD (charge coupled devices) and CMOS (complementary metal oxide semiconductors) units, processing speed, and battery life, have also made digital photography a more reliable solution for professionals.

The power of the dollar

Another big factor in the popularity increase of digital photography is the drop in cost. While the cost of the upper crust of digital cameras is currently in the thousands of dollars, most consumer-level digital cameras cost only a few hundred dollars. In addition, manufacturers offer a wider range of lower-cost products with a good selection of options and benefits. As you can imagine, this led to better prices and more tailored fits that meet the needs of a large number of photographers.

Digital vs. film

In the past, we would have had to tell you that film is far superior to anything digital cameras can muster. However, over the last two or three years, we've seen extreme advances in the quality and sheer volume of information a digital camera can capture. Indeed, today it's possible to take a digital photo that rivals a photo on film. And in the near future, we're sure you'll see parity between the two. But to understand how these two mediums relate, let's take a look at the difference in technologies.

How traditional film images are captured

We've all taken pictures using a regular film camera. However, you might not have thought about how the image is recorded. It's just sort of a natural thing. But to understand how digital photography works, it's good to know how an image is captured on film as well as how it's captured digitally.

Standard photography film is comprised of a special celluloid material coated with photoreactive chemicals. On one side of this celluloid is a gelatin layer than contains micro grains of silver-halide crystals. These light-sensitive grains are the heart of film photography.

When you take a picture using a regular point-and-shoot camera, the light is transferred through the lens onto the film plane. When the light hits the film, the light causes a chemical change to the film, much like the sunlight causes a chemical change to the pigment in your skin giving you a tan (or bad sunburn if you aren't wearing plenty of sunscreen). In the case of film, the silver-halide grains on the film are altered. The greater the exposure to light, the greater the number of silver-halide grains changed. The less the light exposure, the fewer the number of silver-halide grains changed. The latent image is stored on the media, ready for developing.

During the developing process, the surface of the celluloid undergoes a number of chemical reactions. Rather than bore you with the details, suffice it to say that the developing process leaves you with a transparent negative of

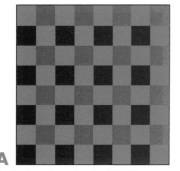

A

By filtering colors using the GRGB Bayer pattern, the photo diodes can transfer light intensities into colors.

B

Separate sensors can separate colors of the same object.

the image. To print the pictures, light is then sent through the negative on to paper coated with color-sensitive layers. Again, you introduce chemistry magic to set the image onto the paper and you have a color print.

As you can see, this method of photography can be costly and time-consuming, especially if you want to do your own processing and printing. And if you want to post your picture to the Web or send it to someone via email, you'd then need to scan the image, which would reduce its quality.

How digital images are captured

A digital camera doesn't require film to capture images. Instead, the light is transferred through the lens onto electronic sensors that convert the light to electrical charges. These sensors are either charge coupled devices (CCD) or complementary metal oxide semiconductors (CMOS). Though they differ slightly in composition and characteristics, they both work similarly. CMOS sensors are becoming more popular, since they currently offer better resolution, use less energy, and allow for on-board image processing.

Each sensor contains an array of light-sensitive diodes that convert light into electrons. The brighter the light, the more electrical charge the diode will produce. The problem is, the diodes can't make out colors, only differing light levels. For

general purposes, a diode is one pixel of an image.

To convert the light into colors, filters are used over the diode to break the light into red, green, or blue. However, since that would drastically reduce the resolution that the sensor is able to capture, the chip designers instead placed the diodes in the pattern shown in Figure A. This pattern, known as the *GRGB Bayer filter pattern*, captures the color of the individual diodes and then comes up with a color based on the adjacent colors. You'll notice that the filter doesn't contain an equal number of each color. Since the eye isn't as sensitive to some colors as others, the pattern must include almost twice as many green pixels.

With each of the three colors captured by separate sensors, you end up with three separate pictures, as illustrated in Figure B. When these three images are layered internally, the camera ends up with a single image. However, as you can see from the example in Figure C, the resolution isn't what you'd expect. To produce the final results, the image must be run through a demosaicing algorithm that combines the color values of each pixel and its eight adjacent pixels into a single 24-bit color value, as shown in Figure D.

The light that represents the analog image is therefore transferred onto the sensor. There the value of light is recorded by photosites that measure red, green, or blue, and then the light is converted into

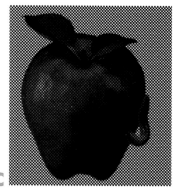

C

The combined colors still show a mosaic pattern that's unacceptable for a photo.

D

Once the image goes through an algorithm to get rid of the mosaic effect, the picture appears normal. You can even see the spots on the worm!

a digital value—the number representing the value of the electronic charge from the diode.

Grains vs. megapixels

To capture an image on film, spectral sensitizers are added to the surface to make the grains of silver-halide crystals sensitive to blue, green, and red light. The method of attaching these sensitizers can alter the size of the crystals on the film. The results can be a fine-grain, which yields a better end photo but is less light sensitive, or a larger grain, which provides better low-light capabilities but produces an image of poorer quality. This sensitivity is the concept behind photographic film speed (ISO or ASA ratings).

Pixels are the digital version of silver-halide crystals. The more pixels a sensor has, the better relative image you can capture. So, instead of shopping for film with a low ASA rating (a film that's less sensitive to light and which has a finer grain), you would look for a camera that captures a larger number of pixels.

Though there's no direct equivalency between grain or film speed and pixel count, it's typically accepted that you need at least a 3.34 megapixel camera to rival a 35 mm image printed to a 4 x 6 format. However, since most digital images end up living on the Web or on the hard drive, the value isn't as important. After all, an image that's 2,080 by 1,542 pixels would be too large to display on the typical computer monitor. You'd actually have to reduce the size of the image just to get it on one screen.

This highlights an important point. If you're only going to be capturing images for the Web, a digital camera with a lower megapixel count will suffice. However, you won't have the flexibility to produce crisp enlargements of the image later. If, on the other hand, you expect to print out many of your images, you'll want to head for the higher end of the megapixel spectrum.

Introduction to a digital camera

Today's digital cameras come in two main formats—the popular point-and-shoot camera and the SLR-form factor, which features more options and the ability to switch lenses. **Figure A** shows examples of each type. Though each varies a bit when it comes to features, they share common elements.

The point-and-shoot is by far the most popular type of digital camera. Most are small and light enough to conveniently keep in your shirt pocket or purse so you're always ready to get that perfect shot. The SLR-type cameras are more bulky, but usually offer higher resolution and additional features not available to the point-and-shoot cameras.

To get the most from your camera, it's important that you understand its capabilities and limitations. And luckily, there's no better way than to get out and take pictures. After all, since you're using a digital camera, you won't have to pay for processing. Just shoot away.

It's also important that you understand how to operate the camera. And unfortunately, this requires a lengthy reading of the manual. Though many of the controls are obvious, there are often subtle features available if you know where to look.

To help you cover the basics, we'll quickly discuss the general components that every camera shares. Keep in mind that the controls we show you in the figures may look different than those on your camera, and indeed, may be located in a different place on your camera. We're simply displaying the controls as examples of the elements on most digital cameras.

Point-and-shoot   **SLR**

A *Traditional digital cameras come in two basic formats.*

The anatomy of a digital camera

Though digital cameras come in various shapes and sizes, all share a number of common elements. Knowing where these elements are located will help you to use your camera more effectively. However, this review is by no means an excuse to avoid reading the user's guide. It would be impossible for us to cover the unique intricacies of each camera here.

Straight on

The following elements are items you'd expect to find on the front of a digital camera, as illustrated in Figure B:

- **Viewfinder.** The first common element is the front of the viewfinder. This is typically a round glass element near the top of the camera. Digital cameras that use the SLR format won't have a viewfinder, since the lens replaces the viewfinder's function. It's important to note that optical viewfinders are notorious for showing less than the entire frame of the picture. In fact, most are offset by as much as 20 percent. When there's a question, go with what you see in the LCD display, not the viewfinder.

- **Autofocus assist light.** In low-light situations, your camera will be unable to focus without some auxiliary light. This assist light flashes in sync with the autofocus mechanism to keep the image from blurring. This light only brightens up to a four or five foot range. Some cameras use an infrared light instead of the visible light.

- **Internal flash.** Virtually every digital camera has an internal flash that allows you to take pictures in low-light settings. The flash element is usually in the center or to the left of the lens.

- **Zoom lens.** Though there are a few special function digital cameras that have a fixed lens, most of the standard cameras have a zoom lens that allows you to tighten in on a subject without getting uncomfortably close. Most of the lenses offer magnification of two to four times the original image.

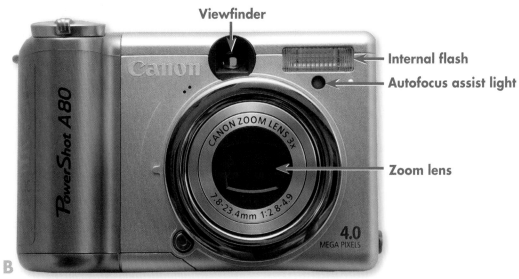

B

These are the common elements on the front of a digital camera.

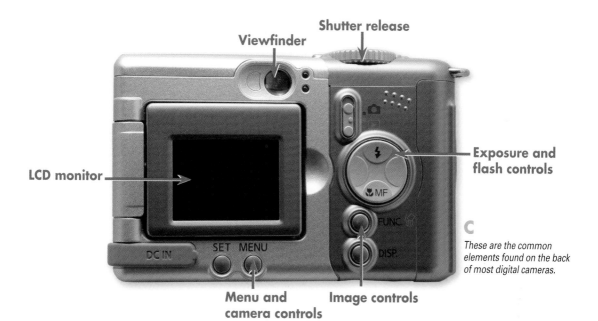

Viewfinder

Shutter release

Exposure and flash controls

LCD monitor

C

These are the common elements found on the back of most digital cameras.

Menu and camera controls

Image controls

Around back

To continue with controls and common elements, here are the items you'd expect to find on the back of a digital camera, as illustrated in Figure C:

- **Exposure and flash controls.** These elements allow you to turn the internal flash on and off, as well as control the power of the flash (i.e., macro, portrait, indoors, scenic settings).

- **Electronic hot shoe.** This option is appearing more frequently on new models, as it provides additional flash possibilities. With this mount, you can attach external flash or slave units. External flashes usually have longer range and better battery life than the internal flash unit.

- **Viewfinder.** This is the business end of the viewfinder. Again, remember that what

you see in this window isn't always all that you'll get in your photo.

- **Shutter release.** Since most digital cameras use autofocus, you must have some way to activate the system. Normally, depressing the shutter release halfway down activates the autofocus and prepares the camera to take the photo. To take the picture, you then continue to press the button a bit harder, or fully down. Some of the SLR-format cameras include an additional shutter release at the bottom-left of the camera. This makes taking portrait-formatted pictures easier.

- **Menu and camera controls.** Though each camera is different, most have menu and camera controls on the back of the camera. These items allow you to configure the

camera and set your individual preferences.

- **Image controls.** If you aren't satisfied with an image, most cameras have a control that allows you to delete the photo instantly. That way you don't fill up your storage card with unwanted photos. Also, there's usually a control in the same area that allows you to review previous images.

- **LCD monitor.** The LCD on the back of a digital camera allows you to review and preview photos. It can also act as a large viewfinder, if you wish. Most LCD monitors are between 1.5 and 2.0 inches diagonally and have an anti-reflective coating to improve the ability to view the monitor in direct sunlight. Some cameras allow you to flip out the LCD monitor to make low- and high-angle shots easier to take.

From the top

Though camera manufacturers have different approaches to the placement and function of their controls, Figure D shows elements that you'd expect to find on the top of the camera. They are as follows:

- **Zoom control.** As we mentioned earlier, most digital cameras have 2x to 4x zoom capability. The zoom control button at the top of the camera allows you to zoom in or out on a subject. In the middle of the control, you may also find the shutter release.

- **Exposure setting control.** Most cameras have various program modes that help you take the very best pictures possible. Usually, this control is a rotating button on the top of the camera. Some cameras choose the middle of this control, rather than the zoom control, for the shutter release.

- **On/Off button.** This button simply turns the camera on and off. To extend battery life, you have to hold the on/off button down for a few seconds to turn it on. That way, you don't accidentally activate the camera.

Zoom control

On/Off button **Exposure setting control**

D

These are the common elements you'd find on the top of most digital cameras.

Understanding resolution settings

Applications: Adobe® Photoshop® 7/CS, Adobe Photoshop Elements 2, or other image-editing application

The concept of resolution can be confusing because there are so many ways that the term can be defined. Some people talk about resolution in terms of an image's spatial resolution—such as saying, "This image is 640 x 480." Others think about resolution more in terms of megabytes—such as saying, "This image is 10 MB and has enough resolution for this output process." But resolution doesn't have to be confusing. By following a few simple rules, you can be sure to get the right resolution for your imaging needs.

The basics

In the most basic sense, *image resolution* is the ability of a digital image to mimic the original scene. However, when most people talk about image resolution, they're referring to *spatial resolution*, or the number of pixels in an image. Although that's what we'll be discussing, it's important to note that there are other types of image resolution. Brightness and color resolution also need to be considered when assessing the quality of an image.

We'll focus on spatial resolution because it's the most noticeable component of image quality. The spatial resolution of an image is determined by the size of the camera's CCD. A digital camera looks at a scene and then samples it into a rectangular array of brightness values that correspond to values in the scene. The higher the rate of sampling, the more image detail, or pixels, that's generated.

The basic unit of an image is a picture element, or *pixel*. The pixel squares make up a large grid that forms an image, such as the one you see in Figure A.

Getting the most resolution

Getting the resolution you need starts with choosing the right camera. The number of pixels required for each application varies, so you should choose a camera based on the largest resolution you'll need.

Camera confusion

When choosing a digital camera, pay special attention to the actual resolution. Many digital camera makers overstate the capabilities of their cameras and confuse the issue by emphasizing megapixels over true resolution information.

A

Pixels are the most basic element of any digital image.

For example, one company advertises their 3.1 megapixel camera as being capable of making images for 11-x-14-inch prints. Of course, any camera is capable of making 11-x-14-inch prints, but whether those images are any good is another story altogether. In the case of the 3.1 megapixel camera, if you dig into this camera's specs for its actual spatial resolution of 2160 x 1440, you'll find that this resolution isn't optimal for an 11-x-14-inch print.

You can't get there from here

You can test this for yourself by plugging the pixel numbers into an image-editing application. By doing so, you'll be able to see what the actual image size of these numbers works out to be. We'll show you how it's done.

We'll be using Photoshop or Photoshop Elements for this example, but you can use just about any image-editing program to run this test. To do so:

1. Launch Photoshop or Photoshop Elements and then choose File ▸ New to open the New dialog box.

2. Set the Width and Height units to Pixels and then enter *2160* in the Width text box and *1440* in the Height text box.

3. Click OK and your new document opens.

4. Choose Image ▸ Image Size (Image ▸ Resize ▸ Image Size in Photoshop Elements) to open the Image Size dialog box shown in Figure B. As you can see, our image is currently 20 x 30 inches at 72 dpi.

This digital image has a set maximum number of pixels, but you can change how those pixels are distributed. As we mentioned earlier, the manufacturer says this camera is capable of producing an 11-x-14-inch image. To test this statement:

1. Enter *14* in the Width text box—the Height and Resolution change automatically if they're linked.

2. If they aren't linked, deselect the Resample Image check box to link them and re-enter *14* in the Width text box. Either way, the Height displays as 9.333 inches with a Resolution of 154.286 pixels/inch. For home printing, you'll find that a measurement of 250 to 300 pixels gives you better results, as we'll explain below.

Not only is 154 pixels not enough resolution to get optimal print quality, but you've also probably noticed that the image is only 9.4 x 14, not 11 x 14. This means that you need to make the image larger to make the short side fit the 11-inch dimension. This is

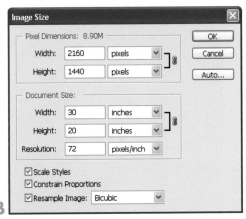

B

The Image Size dialog box shows you how many pixels are distributed in an image of a specified size.

because the aspect ratio of the CCD doesn't accommodate the traditional 11-x-14-inch print format. If you wanted to produce an 11-x-14-inch print from this image, you'd have to set the Height to 11, which would then make the Width 16.5 inches with a final resolution of 130.909 pixels-per-inch. Next, you'd have to crop the width of your picture to fit into the 11 x 14 format.

As you can see, a 3.1 megapixel camera won't produce optimum results at 11 x 14. Even a 5 megapixel camera doesn't have quite enough resolution to support this print size. However, software and inkjet printer technologies are changing to make this possible.

Aspect ratio

Part of the resolution problem comes about because of the differences in aspect ratios between digital devices and film. Computer monitors, CCDs, etc., use the VGA aspect ratio of 4:3. Traditional 35 mm has an aspect ratio of 2:3, which allows you to get full frame prints on 4-x-6-inch paper. Since a CCD is in the 4:3 aspect ratio, it actually creates a 4.5-x-6-inch print, which means you always have to trim a ½ inch off the height of your image if you want to stick to a traditional print size. For larger print sizes, both digital and traditional images usually require cropping to fit 8 x 10 or 11 x 14. **Figure C** shows the difference between these two aspect ratios.

Digital zoom

Another camera factor that can reduce the quality of your images is using the digital zoom feature. This function essentially just crops from the center of an image. It doesn't actually help you capture any additional detail in the scene. Better cameras take the cropped capture and then interpolate the image back to the camera's native resolution. However, not all cameras do this. We recommend disabling the digital zoom on your camera and using software to make cropping adjustments so you don't inadvertently take images with too little resolution.

From pixels to dots

Working with printers is another area where people can get confused about resolution, because pixels have to convert to dots or a line screen. Whether you're printing out an image on your home printer or trying to prepare images for press, it's important to understand your final output device and give it the correct amount of information. Too much data slows down the process, while not enough may give you poor image quality. We'll show you how to determine the right resolution for your home printer and for the press.

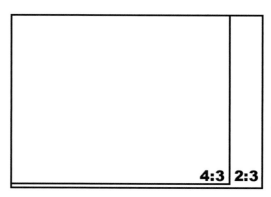

C

Aspect ratios of film and digital devices are different, making it more difficult to fit images taken with digital cameras into standard print sizes.

Determining dpi (dots per inch) for inkjet

People frequently ask questions such as, "My printer has a resolution of 1200 dpi; does my image need to be at 1200 dpi too?" The answer is no. Printers have special algorithms that break down an image into dots. If you have a color image at 300 dpi that's going to be printed on a four-color photo printer capable of 1200 dpi, then you have 300 w being printed by each color print head—a total of 1200 dpi. A resolution of 300 dpi is ideal for this situation, but you may find that you can get away with slightly lower resolutions, such as 250 dpi.

However, technology is always changing. Some printers are capable of greater color depth per pixel, such as the CREt-enabled (Color Resolution Enhancement technology) Hewlett-Packard photo printers.

In theory, these printers allow you to generate a high-quality image from a low-resolution file by increasing the number of ink drops per pixel.

Resolution in Web development

It's commonly recommended for people to buy a cheap digital camera if their main intention is to just put images on the Web. Cheap cameras are considered adequate for Web work because your images typically never need to be larger than 640 x 480.

However, cheap cameras aren't cheap solely because they have smaller CCDs. They also have a variety of other cheaper components, which can affect image quality. In **Figure D**, you can see the results of a test of two cameras made by the same manufacturer. Both images were shot at 640 x 480. Though the resolution is the same, the sharpness, color rendition, and dynamic range of the more expensive camera yields a far better image.

If you were trying to sell this product, which do you think would generate better sales? The difference between these images is even more evident online than it is in print. In online marketing, the way you present your products can make or break your company. Don't shoot yourself in the foot by buying a cheap camera. The better cameras can usually shoot at multiple resolutions. So, you'll not only be able to take better pictures for the Web, but you'll also have the benefit of owning a camera that's able to generate images for print as well.

High-end consumer camera

Low-end consumer camera

D

Which image would you rather have on your Web page?

Understanding color depth

The importance of color depth in image quality is a concept that's fuzzy to many people who work with digital images. They hear terms like *bit depth* and *color depth*, and they know they relate to each other in some manner, but they aren't sure how. We'll clear up any uncertainty by showing you how image quality, color depth, and bits are intertwined with the image types you work with frequently, such as RGB, grayscale, and Indexed images.

The basics of bits

The color depth of an image is also referred to as bit depth. A *bit* is the smallest unit of data a computer uses to store information. It's the basic machine language of a computer for all functions and is also called the *Binary number system*.

A bit can have a value of either 1 (on) or 0 (off). In terms of images, this would generate a purely black and white image, which is frequently referred to as a *bitmap*. You can see a 1-bit image in **Figure A**. The image appears to have some tone based on the proximity of the pixels, but each pixel is either black or white.

As you increase the number of bits per pixel, you increase the available tones you can generate. In **Table A**, you can see a summary of common bit values and the available colors for each pixel. As you can see, the color possibilities increase exponentially as the number of

bits increases. If you allocate 2 bits per pixel, then you can have four potential tones and so on. We'll show you how this applies to 8-bit grayscale images.

Grayscale images

CMYK, RGB, and grayscale images are based on channels, which are 8-bit grayscale images. In the case of a grayscale image, like the one in **Figure B** on the next page, the image and its single channel are identical. All grayscale images are 8-bit, which means they can have up to 256 tones.

A

A 1-bit image consists of only black and white pixels.

Table A: *Color values increase exponentially as more bits are allocated.*

Bit depth	Available colors
1 bit	2 colors
2 bits	4 colors
4 bits	16 colors
5 bits	32 colors
6 bits	64 colors
7 bits	128 colors
8 bits	256 colors

When you have 8 bits per pixel, you have 256 possible combinations of 0s and 1s in which to numerically describe a tone. Black is stored as 00000000, while white is stored as 11111111. All other tones are some numeric combination in between. What you can derive from this is that each possible tone of a grayscale image is predefined numerically. As you adjust the contrast of your image, you can manipulate the amount of tone and location of a tone, but you'll never have more than 256 possible tones.

True color

Color images aren't that different from grayscale images. In fact, a color image is just three grayscale images combined. True color images are sometimes referred to as 24-bit because they're composed of three 8-bit images, one for each of the RGB color channels. When the three channels are superimposed over each other, you get a true color image like the one shown in Figure C.

In numeric terms, true color is more than 16 million colors because it's 2^{24}, or 2 x 2 x 2 x 2 x … (24 times), which equals 16.7 million colors. That's a phenomenal number of tones to work with—and yet sometimes you may want even more.

Indexed images

The GIF format commonly used for Web graphics is also limited to 256 tones, but it's different from a grayscale image. GIF images don't have channels. Instead of a channel, a color lookup table (CLUT) defines the GIF's tonal range. If you open a GIF image in Adobe Photoshop and click on the Channels palette, you'll see a layer labeled Index instead of a channel. Instead of a predefined grayscale table as described by a channel, each color in a GIF color table can be selected individually, but the same

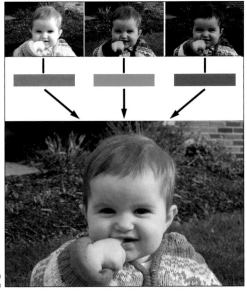

B

Grayscale images can only have 256 tones.

C

True color, or 24-bit, images are made up of three 8-bit images.

principles of bit depth still hold true. A 1-bit GIF image has two colors, but those colors don't need to be black and white. In Figure D, you can see how the number of bits directly affects the representation of an image.

Experimenting with GIF settings is a good way to learn about color depth. The GIF format compresses color images by removing color variety, so instead of millions of colors, you only have 256. You can also GIF-compress grayscale images, but since they only have 256 tones to begin with, there will be no visual change from indexing them unless you compress them as something smaller than 8-bit.

Hardware bit depth

Monitors, scanners, and digital cameras are all affected by bit depth. While perusing this section, one thing to keep in mind is that even though devices like scanners and digital cameras are capable of capturing at higher bit depths, the printing industry, software, and computers have more or less standardized 24-bit color. Even though you can work with images with higher bit depths, you'll eventually need to bring it down to 24-bit for output.

Monitors

Monitors mix red, green, and blue phosphors to produce colors in a process known as *spatial integration*. A video card controls the available colors on a monitor. The typical monitor usually has a video card capable of 24-bit or millions of colors. Sometimes, you'll see monitors or video cards for 32-bit display,

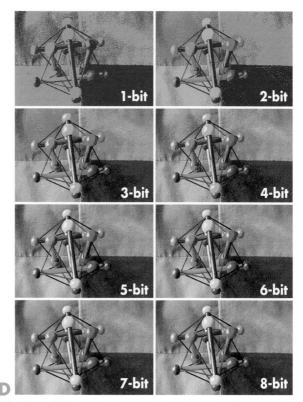

D

Like a channel, GIF compression maps colors to bits. But, unlike a channel, you can pick those colors yourself.

but in reality, only 24 of those bits are for color. The other eight are typically null and used to enhance monitor speed or other functions.

Scanners

Like digital cameras, scanners also capture images with a CCD. One of the most important things to know about a scanner before you buy it is its bit depth. For example, many Epson scanners have 48-bit color, which is 16 bits per channel. This means they can capture trillions of colors. Depending on the scanner and scanning software you use, you may be able to bring a high-bit image directly into Photoshop or the scanner software might automatically resample to 24 bits. In either case, a 48-bit scanner gives you a greater chance of capturing critical highlight and shadow detail than a 36-bit or lower model.

Digital cameras

Whereas the bit depth of scanners is heavily touted, the bit depth of consumer digital cameras rarely is. They're typically advertised as 24-bit, even if they happen to have higher bit depths for capture.

Like scanners, many digital cameras are actually capturing at higher bit depths and then resampling to 24-bit internally. This might sound a little strange, but as with scanners, this method actually provides better color information than if a camera captured at 24-bit directly. The more bits you have per sample, the more accurate color rendition the device is able to render. For digital cameras, this especially affects a camera's ability to pick up shadow detail, but the overall dynamic range of the image improves with more bits.

Professional digital cameras usually capture and save out files of higher bit depths. This gives you the opportunity to resample the image to 24-bit yourself using proprietary software or Photoshop. We expect the ability to save out files of higher bit depths will eventually work its way down to consumer-level cameras.

Software support of bit depth

Photoshop supports multiple bit depths from 1-bit to 16-bit per channel images, with normal images being 8 bits per channel. If you have 16 bits per channel, this results in a 64-bit CMYK file, a 48-bit RGB file, or a 16-bit grayscale file. Presently, only a fraction of Photoshop's functions, such as Levels, Curves, and basic transformations, are available for 16-bit manipulation, although Photoshop CS has expanded support greatly.

Why work with high-bit depth?

Anytime you work with high-bit images, such as 10 bits per channel or 12 bits per channel, Photoshop throws them into the 16 bits per channel category, which is used for any image larger than 8 bits per channel. Even though high-bit depth images have large file sizes and are somewhat unwieldy, it's much better to use them to perform tonal correction with Curves, Levels, and the like because you have more tones to work with and you're less likely to compress (and lose) highlight and shadow detail. Once you've

E

CMYK grayscale images have more tonality but also a potential for color casts.

made your Gamma adjustments, you can then convert to 8 bits per channel for further manipulation.

Printing and color depth

Bit depth also affects images when you print them. Most printers are set up for using the four basic inks (cyan, magenta, yellow, black), one for each channel in a CMYK image. Some printers enhance their color depth by including additional colors, such as light cyan and light magenta, to increase the accuracy of depicting color. Other printers produce more dots per pixel, allowing greater control over tonality. Some do both.

Bit depth really comes into play with the printing of grayscale images. If you print a beautiful black and white image on your color printer, it won't look that great because a single ink on a printer isn't capable of rendering all the possible tonality in a grayscale image. Much like increasing bit depth to achieve more colors, increasing inks will give you more tone. To get better image quality for grayscale images, you need to convert them to print in CMYK or invest in a quadtone (four-color black) ink system. You'll get vastly superior results printing with multiple inks rather than one.

The press

Increasing tonality through ink isn't true for just desktop printers. The setting choices you make for images that you send to print professionally are important as well. For example, an 8-bit grayscale image won't get nearly the ink coverage that printing a grayscale image in CMYK will get you. As shown in Figure E, we printed the same image shown in Figure B, but this image has different tonality because four inks are being used to render the image rather than one. As you can see, we changed an image by changing its color depth but not its resolution.

Digital SLR

Are you considering upgrading to a digital single lens reflex (DSLR) camera? Or perhaps you're just curious about what makes them so great. With prices dropping and exciting new DSLR models being released, it's difficult not to be tempted by their advanced capabilities and excellent image quality. But with the influx of options and rapidly changing world of digital technology, it's hard to tell whether to stick with a compact point-and-shoot model or upgrade to the greater flexibility of a DSLR, such as the Nikon D2H shown in Figure A.

Is a DSLR right for you?

You'll need to assess how and what you photograph to see if a DSLR is right for you. If your photography takes you to challenging locations, a DSLR typically has a more durable build quality to survive those bumps along the road. If you want to have the maximum flexibility over aspects like depth of field, aperture, and shutter speed (capabilities that are somewhat stunted on most digital cameras), a DSLR is going to offer a wider range of exposure options.

Interchangeable lenses

The biggest benefit with DSLR cameras is the ability to change your lens, giving you more versatility when shooting. Most are designed to use the same lenses as film cameras, which makes it

attractive for photographers who have invested lots of money in a set of lenses. While there is a new breed of lenses designed especially for digital cameras, most of the time these lenses are interchangeable. It's important to understand that these lenses are primarily used to project onto a 35 mm frame, but image sensors are usually two-thirds of this size, as illustrated in Figure B. This causes the focal length of the lens to increase by 1.5 times, a number commonly referred to as the *focal multiplier*. If you're shooting with a 200 mm lens on a DSLR, the focal length multiplier makes it act like a 300 mm lens. This is good news for those who like to shoot faraway objects, as zoom lenses can be very expensive. However, it limits a DSLR's ability to shoot at wide angles, as a 24 mm lens acts like a 35 mm lens, limiting your field of view.

Image sensors

Typically, the image sensors in DSLR cameras are larger and can produce superior image quality. As we mentioned, the size of a typical digital camera sensor is usually only a fraction of the size of a 35 mm frame, but some DSLRs have sensors that are of equal size (known as *full-frame* sensors). While most image sensors are around 6 megapixels in DSLR cameras, there's a range of image sensors available. Make sure you match your image sensor with your intended output and don't

A

The 4 megapixel Nikon D2H is a popular DSLR camera typically aimed at professional photographers, but many digital camera enthusiasts are beginning to consider upgrading.

just go for the biggest sensor available.

Note: Keep in mind that the size of the sensor is going to affect the focal multiplier for your lenses and influence your ability to frame your shots.

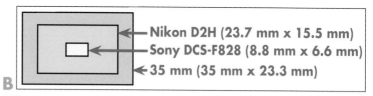

B

While there are a few full-frame sensors, most digital camera image sensors are much smaller than a 35 mm frame.

Exposure system

One of the biggest limitations of point-and-shoot digital cameras is their narrow aperture range. With a DSLR, the range is much wider and usually only limited to the lenses you use. This allows for a more controllable depth of field so you can better control what elements of your scene are in focus. As for shutter speeds, expect much slower and much faster shutter speeds than you'll find on a point-and-shoot digital camera. You'll also find a more accurate metering system that can react to a wide range of lighting situations and help you capture more accurate exposures. Finally, DSLR cameras have more ISO settings you can choose from, often ranging from ISO 100 to ISO 1600 (and beyond on the higher end models).

Focus system

The professional nature of a DSLR requires that they use the fastest, most accurate focus systems available. Of course, manual focus is part of the package, but a fast and precise autofocus system is crucial for shooting fast-moving action, such as sports. When evaluating autofocus capabilities, look for models that offer selectable focus modes (such as, single shot AF or continuous tracking AF) so you can fine-tune the camera to your shooting situation.

Shot speed

Another consideration is how long you have to wait before you take another picture. DSLRs usually have much faster refresh rates and higher image buffers to allow the photographer to take more images per sequence. While most reach a maximum of 3 or 4 frames per second, this number is increasing rapidly and should match their film counterparts soon. DSLRs also offer a short shutter lag, which is the delay between when the shutter button is pressed and the image is captured, making it easier to more accurately time your shots.

Other considerations

As you research these cameras, you'll find other features and options that interest you. Get a hold of some cameras and see how they feel. Check out the different user interfaces and make sure you feel comfortable with making adjustments. Find out which accessories are available for each model and ensure that you'll have a wide range of lens options to choose from. Purchasing a DSLR is an investment, so do your homework and find the one that best meets your needs.

Connecting your camera to your computer

Once you've captured a collection of great photos, you'll want to transfer them to your computer. Though nearly every camera manufacturer uses their own software to transfer pictures from their camera to the computer, the same general concepts apply to all of them.

Early digital cameras relied on serial connections for transferring images from the digital camera to the computer. Since the serial port isn't known for its high-speed transfers, it could take a while to move your pictures from the camera to the computer. These days, however, most cameras use USB or FireWire® for their connectivity needs.

To connect your camera to your computer, first locate the data transfer port on the camera, as shown in Figure A. This port is usually hidden by a rubber cover to protect it from dirt and the elements. Though the connections are always labeled for your convenience, you really won't need to look for them, since the cables will only fit in one of the ports (other ports included on your camera may be a video out and power).

USB

USB is a very capable method of transfer since you can move data at about 350 KB/second. But as you move up in the digital camera food chain, and find yourself shooting with a 15-megapixel camera, you'll want more. That's because a single image can be more than 5 MB in size. Try to transfer a card full of files this size and you'll be longing for a FireWire connection.

USB 2.0

A new standard, USB 2.0, promises to improve not only the download speeds from digital cameras, but also allow better integration with other digital devices. USB 2.0 supports theoretical speeds of up to 480 Mbps, which is about 40 times faster than USB 1.x. The speed improvement will allow USB users to take advantage of faster downloads and shorten downtime from shooting.

A

Most cameras use a USB connection (the one in the middle) to transfer data to a computer.

Another important feature of USB 2.0 is backward-compatibility. USB 2.0 is fully backward-compatible with USB 1.1 peripherals. In fact, USB hub specifications were changed to allow this, such that USB hubs must recognize and be able to communicate with both USB version 1.1 and 2.0 peripherals.

FireWire

FireWire connections (also called IEEE 1394) are usually included on higher-end digital and video cameras. They can transfer data at almost five times that of USB, but they aren't as popular as USB.

FireWire currently supports data transfer rates of up to 400 Mbps and 800 Mbps. However, plans are in the works for a new version that supports speeds of up to 1.2 Gbps. There's considerable controversy concerning whether USB or FireWire is the superior technology, but it really depends on the device you need to connect. FireWire tends to be preferred for digital video cameras and high-end scanners, while peripheral devices, such as keyboards and digital cameras, use USB connections.

Fire up the software

Once you've connected your camera to your computer, you simply turn on the camera, launch the software, and initiate the transfer. When you do, the software will poll the camera to determine the number and size of files being transferred, and then begin moving them from the camera to the computer. Once the transfer is complete, we'd suggest you preview the images before you do anything else. It's especially important to make sure that the transfer moved all your photos over to the computer. Once you know that all the files have been copied to the computer, you can delete the files from the camera.

Lens converters

Just understanding the basics isn't enough if you really want to take full advantage of your digital camera. To really get the most out of the camera, and get great pictures along the way, you may want to invest in a few accessories that will make your camera complete.

Most digital cameras come with a reasonable zoom range—usually between 2x and 4x. But your creative spirit might yearn for something more—or something different. When that's the case, you may look at adding a lens converter to your camera. These attachments allow you to change the focal length of your built-in lens. To attach the

converter, shown in Figure A, all you do is screw it on to the end of the existing lens (which may require a step-down ring). There are usually four different focal lengths available in most converter sets: fish-eye or ultra-wide angle, wide angle, telephoto, and macro. Attached, the converters can drastically change the composition of a picture.

As you can see from the sample photo shown in Figure B, a wide-angle lens can give a photo an entirely different perspective. Unfortunately, these lenses aren't cheap. A single converter can run into the hundreds of dollars.

A

Lens converters can extend the focal length of the built-in lens.

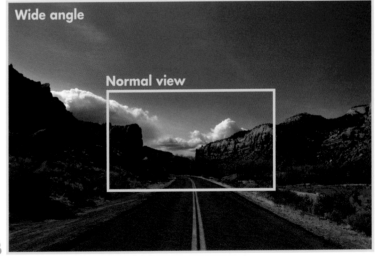

B

Adding a wide-angle converter to your digital arsenal can change the perspective of your photos.

Rechargeable batteries

Good batteries are by far the best accessories you can add to your digital camera arsenal. If you're lucky, your camera came with its own charger and battery—otherwise, you'll need to purchase your own rechargeable batteries and charger. Sure, buying the traditional alkaline batteries may be the cheapest way to go up front, but if you've ever taken this approach, you know that these batteries quickly run dry and need replacing often. For those reasons, investing in good rechargeable batteries is a must, even if you only use your digital camera sparingly.

Sources of energy

When you start exploring your options for rechargeable batteries, your first stop should be your camera's user's manual. Not only does it specify what size and voltage is needed, but it also recommends batteries that work best with your particular camera.

The recommendation will, most likely, come in the form of an expensive proprietary battery. Investigate this battery's specs and see if you can find a cheaper battery with similar specs made by another company. You'll probably find yourself looking at one or more different types of batteries. But be careful! If damage is done to your camera as a result of the non-proprietary battery, the manufacturer may not honor your warranty. Here are some of the most common batteries used in digital cameras:

- **NiMH.** Nickel Metal Hydride (NiMH) batteries are the most commonly used batteries in digital cameras. They're relatively inexpensive, are environmentally friendly, and give you a lot of pictures per charging cycle. On the downside, they can only be charged about 500 times before they become unusable. For most scenarios, this is the type of battery that will serve you the best, as they offer consistent power with a short charge time.

- **NiCd.** Although Nickel Cadmium (NiCd) batteries are still the most popular rechargeable batteries overall, they aren't used in digital cameras as often as NiMH batteries. Although they charge quickly and can last through more charging cycles than NiMH batteries, they tend to lose their charge more quickly (meaning fewer shots between recharging). Plus, NiCd batteries respond poorly to the high-power surges that occur when your camera is starting up or processing a file. Perhaps most importantly, the cadmium in the batteries is highly toxic and thus is an environmental nightmare.

- **LiIon.** Ideally, the newer Lithium Ion (LiIon) batteries are your best option.

Their charge can last twice as long as a NiMH battery's charge, they can handle just as many charging cycles as a NiMH battery, and they don't lose their charge as quickly when sitting on a shelf. Unfortunately, these benefits come at a much higher price and often come in a battery size that isn't designed for your camera. However, keep your eyes open and contact the company if your camera is being ignored. Most likely, a configuration to suit your needs is on its way.

Prolonging a battery's charge and lifespan

Whichever type of rechargeable battery you decide to use, there are several ways to prolong its charge and its overall lifespan. They are as follows:

- Be sure not to overcharge your batteries—which is the leading cause of death among rechargeable batteries. Look for a "smart" battery charger, which means it comes equipped with a sensor that moderates the current to the battery to help alleviate this problem.

- Condition your batteries (fully drain and recharge them) for optimal performance. Do this when you first buy the bat-

teries and then once every 50 to 100 charge cycles. For the best and safest results, use a charger with conditioning features built in.

- Turn off autofocus when you aren't using it—leaving it on forces the camera to attempt to focus every time you point the lens in a different direction, wasting battery power.

- Don't zoom or focus on objects unnecessarily. This also drains the battery.

- Use the optical viewfinder instead of the LCD monitor, or at least turn off the color mode or turn down the brightness. This feature can draw an enormous amount of energy from your batteries.

- Use an AC adapter whenever possible, especially when displaying images, printing images, or downloading them to a computer.

- If you don't anticipate using the camera for an extended period of time, remove the batteries and store them in a cool, dry place. Be sure to let them warm back up to room temperature before using them again—warmth speeds up the chemical processes in the batteries, making them much more efficient.

Tripods

Any digital photographer aiming to get high-quality images is going to need a tripod at some point. While fast shutter speeds can eliminate some of the natural shakiness of our world, using a tripod for camera stability offers ultimate control over the crispness of your shots. You may think your shooting style doesn't require a firm support, but you'd be surprised at how a quality tripod can reduce vibration and result in sharper digital images.

Automatically blurry

The automatic features of your digital camera might be working against you. If you're shooting in a low-light environment or have elected to turn the flash off, your camera will try to compensate by either increasing the shutter speed or opening the aperture to allow more light in. If you aren't steady during these longer exposures, blurring occurs. While the LCD preview on most cameras can allow you to catch this problem early, wouldn't you rather get the shot right the first time? Also, setting your camera manually can help, but you might miss that perfect shot while you're busy messing around with your camera's menu.

A common problem

We're referring primarily to digital cameras, but most of the problems that can be solved by using a tripod apply to all types of photography. You wouldn't get very far taking a shot at night using a long exposure without a stable surface to shoot on. Freezing high-speed action or using your zoom lens gets even trickier when you're moving as well. Even shooting simple product shots for an online auction can benefit from a steady shot.

Choosing your tripod

When choosing a tripod for a digital camera, there are a number of questions you should ask. First, what are you using the tripod for? If you're going to be in a studio shooting digital images all day, you'll want to get a heavy, sturdy model with a flexible range of positioning. If you're a photographer who usually shoots outdoors, you'll want a lighter tripod that can handle the elements and that's easy to carry.

Second, how much do you want to spend? Tripod costs range from $15 for stripped-down versions to $1,000 and up for professional models. There are several good-quality models available for under $100. While this might still sound like a lot, consider that a good tripod should last you a lifetime. In a technological era where digital cameras are "obsolete" after two years, a well-made tripod is useful forever.

Third, how much weight do you want to carry around? With the diminutive nature of today's digital cameras, do you want to lug around a big clunker of a tripod? While weight certainly contributes to the overall stability of the tripod, try to find a middle ground that meets your need for strength but doesn't break your back. Tripods made from composite materials usually offer the best balance of strength and weight.

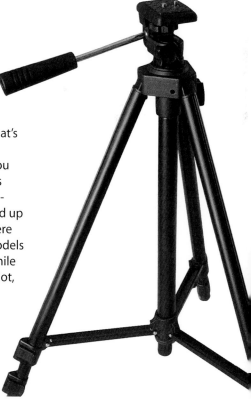

Digital film cards and card readers

The myriad of digital image file storage options available for digital camera users today can be overwhelming. In many cases, the type of removable media you prefer determines the brand of camera you buy. As storage capacities increase and the designs of media types diversify, it's important to keep up to date on the latest in storage technology. Knowing the advantages and disadvantages of storage technology helps ensure that your choice meets your needs. Here are some of the common storage technologies:

- **CompactFlash® Type I.** The first storage option we'll discuss, CF Type I media, is one of the most popular types of storage media on the market. This familiar format has a maximum storage capacity in the gigabtyes, with many other capacity increments available. The biggest benefit of CompactFlash cards is their flexibility. These cards can be used with any camera that has a CF Type I slot, regardless of the capacity or brand of the card. CompactFlash cards also can be easily used in other media-related devices, such as MP3 players and PDAs. The price range for CompactFlash cards varies tremendously. More standard cards in the 32 MB to 256 MB range are reasonably priced (under $100), while the higher capacity cards carry a premium price in the $400 to $500 range.

- **SmartMedia™.** Next up is SmartMedia, which is popular with many camera manufacturers. SmartMedia cards are smaller than credit cards and are just about as thin. Their small size, as shown in Figure A, belies their storage capabilities, with maximum configurations weighing in at 128 MB. The diminutive size of the card is due to the card controller's placement on the camera, unlike CompactFlash cards, which have the controller on the card itself. The makeup of the SmartMedia card makes for smaller media, but then slightly larger card slots are needed in the body of the camera to accommodate the controller.

- **xD Picture Card™.** The smallest type of storage media for

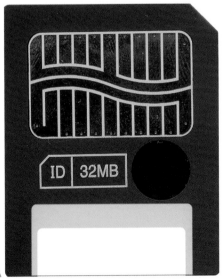

A

The diminutive size of the SmartMedia format is its biggest benefit.

digital cameras is xD Picture Card, which is about as big as the fingernail on your thumb. Developed by Fuji and Olympus to upgrade the limited SmartMedia format, xD is only used on cameras by those manufacturers. With a storage potential of 8 GB, this might be the storage type to watch.

- **Memory Stick®.** The Memory Stick format, invented by Sony, is currently used only in Sony brand products. This storage format looks like a purple stick of gum and is compatible with other Sony digital products, such as digital camcorders and photo printers. There are many megabyte configurations of Memory Sticks, with the largest capacity at 1 GB.

- **CD-R.** One of the more interesting storage innovations is the use of CD-R technology. Also developed by Sony, this storage method allows a 3.5-inch disk to be burned directly in the camera. The 156 MB storage capacity of the inexpensive disks is impressive, but this option is currently only available on select Sony cameras.

- **CompactFlash Type II.** This format is a thicker version of the standard CompactFlash Type I card and uses a specialty slot that can usually read both Type I and Type II formats. The massive storage capacity, ranging from 256 MB to 4 GB, should supply you with free space for quite a while. Hopefully, as the prices of cameras come down, so will the price of these cards. This format had some reliability issues early on, but with many of these problems now solved you can expect to see these cards used in many other cameras.

- **Secure Digital™.** The Secure Digital (SD) format was designed for use with a variety of devices, such as cameras, PDAs, MP3 players, and cellular phones. At about the size of a postage stamp, this format was also made to fit in small places. Another advantage of the SD format is fast write times and low battery consumption, definite selling points for most digital photographers.

Which is best for you?

The best storage method for you really depends on how you shoot, your method of downloading, and, most importantly, your budget. If having the largest possible memory size is important to you (so you can shoot your entire trip to Italy, for example), go with CF Type II media. If it's more important to you to have a format that's extremely flexible, especially if you're using multiple brands of cameras, CompactFlash (Type I) is a smart choice. If you own five other Sony digital devices, it makes sense to go with the Memory Stick. Overall, think about the situations in which you'll be shooting and what equipment you'll be using to capture your images.

Card readers for your memory

Once you've chosen the right memory options for your camera, the next accessory you should consider is a card reader. This item allows you to transfer images from the card to your computer without connecting your camera to your computer. Card readers come in all shapes and sizes.

Most of the readers plug into the USB port of your computer and then have a slot for CompactFlash, SmartMedia, or Memory Stick cards. There are even readers that can read all three types of storage.

Another type of reader, particularly handy for folks with laptops, is the PCMCIA card adapter. This device is little more than a shell for the memory card that you then plug into the PCMCIA slot on your laptop. Your computer will load the memory card on the laptop as a hard drive—you just copy the photos from the card to wherever you like.

Speed is another advantage to using dedicated card readers for transferring photos. The typical camera connection via a USB cable can only transfer data at about 350 KB/second. A USB card reader, on the other hand, can transfer data at 500 KB/second and a PCMCIA card adapter can reach transfer rates of 1,300 KB/second.

Organizing your digital camera equipment

As digital technology improves and camera prices drop, many digital photographers are looking to upgrade, sometimes as often as once or twice a year. Others have a point-and-shoot for everyday use and a more complex model for portraits or landscapes. But with every new camera comes a new set of cables, chargers, batteries, memory cards, and other accessories that can clutter your workspace and make using several cameras a hassle. Since most digital camera manufacturers use proprietary connections and power sources, you'll have to learn to live with a collection of digital camera equipment. However, by getting organized and removing what isn't necessary, you can optimize your workflow and enjoy your multiple digital cameras without the mess.

The curse of the cluttered cables

The cables used to connect your camera and provide power are the main cause of desktop clutter. Almost every digital camera comes with a USB, FireWire, or serial cable to connect the camera to the computer, and almost all can run from an AC adapter to save battery life. Combine just those two cables with your mouse and keyboard cables and your desktop starts to look like a bowl of spaghetti.

Eliminate connection cables

Our recommendation is to immediately remove the connection cables and purchase a card reader. If you have only one media type (such as CompactFlash), you could buy one especially for that format. However, it's best to purchase one of the multiformat units if you have cameras that use different media types. The unit shown in Figure A can read CompactFlash (Type I and II), SmartMedia, SecureDigital, and Memory Stick, and costs about $25. Now you have only one cable with a fast, reliable USB connection that's self-powered and stationary. Buying a multiformat reader also allows you to be flexible with your media types, instead of tying you to one type or another.

So, what do you do with your cables? Of course, you need to save them, but we recommend an additional step. Take the time to label each cable with the name of the camera and connection type, as we have in Figure B on the next page. Then, coil your cables neatly to avoid any unnecessary wear and tear during storage. Cables have a tendency to tangle, so avoid any possible damage by securing your coil with a twist tie or piece of tape. You may feel like you're preparing for a stint at summer camp, but since these cables all look similar, labeling makes it easy to locate the one you need.

A

This multiformat reader allows you to download images from five different storage media types.

Don't get power-mad

Power supplies and chargers are tricky, as they tend to be specific to each camera. Mixing power supplies can cause serious damage, so always approach power issues carefully. One way to reduce the number of power supplies is to buy cameras made by the same manufacturer. Sony and Nikon are good examples of companies that have power supplies and batteries that work safely with multiple camera models, and in the case of Sony, even their line of digital video cameras is compatible. While sticking with one manufacturer may limit your options, it does reduce the clutter. You can also select digital cameras that use non-proprietary rechargeable batteries that can be interchanged between cameras, or investigate external battery pack options. As always, make sure any new power source is fully compatible with your digital camera before plugging it in.

The best of both worlds?

Digital camera systems like Kodak's EasyShare or HP's Photosmart dock combine power and connectivity into one package. Again, you limit yourself to one family of cameras, but these systems can be beneficial in a multiple-camera situation. For example, a real estate agency may purchase several digital cameras and the appropriate docking station. Now the agency has one central location for downloading and charging multiple cameras so their agents can grab an available camera, take their shots, and then return the camera to the dock for both download and charging. Not only is this efficient and a smart financial decision, but it can also reduce the amount of technical help needed to support multiple cameras and computers.

Choose interchangeable add-on lenses

Add-on lenses and filters are useful accessories for a digital camera, but there are several factors to consider when buying them. Since camera lenses vary in size, most add-on lenses and filters require a step-down ring to attach to the camera body. Instead of buying different

B

If you label lesser-used cables, you'll have an easier time finding them when you need them.

sizes of expensive lenses and filters, buy the inexpensive step-down rings to adapt to each camera, which saves both space and money. If you have no choice but to have specific lenses or filters for a particular camera, make sure you keep them labeled as well, but be careful not to obscure the lens or damage it in any way when labeling it.

Save your software

There's a tendency for most Internet-savvy digital photographers to believe that the software and drivers for their cameras will always be on the Internet somewhere. But why take the chance? Companies have no responsibility to keep software online, and may even charge you to download something you already purchased. Keep all of your software, especially the drivers, in one location, and back it up if permissible by the software manufacturer. The purchase of a new computer, the death of an old one, and a trip to see your brother-in-law are all examples of when you'll wish you had your camera software handy. Even though software drivers have become less important with the introduction of inexpensive card readers, they're still a useful link to your camera.

Storage solutions

It's a good idea to designate a central location for your digital camera equipment and keep everything together. The way you keep things organized

C

If you carry around two or more digital cameras, consider using smaller protective cases for each one—they not only protect your camera, but also help you stay organized.

depends on your shooting style, but here are a few tips.

For your actively used equipment, use a good camera bag that provides adequate storage space and above-average protection. You can purchase smaller camera bags that fit the dimensions of your digital camera for an added layer of protection, as shown in **Figure C**. Most of these smaller cases have room to store an extra battery or media. Keeping the accessories close to the camera makes it much easier to locate what you need when you're shooting.

For your storage media, consider buying a special case to hold them when not in use. They keep your media together, and some even have water- and environment-resistant linings that protect your media from harm. You can check out examples of these cases at www.roadwired.com or www.watertightcase.com.

For your lesser-used equipment, find a box or plastic container that's big enough to hold everything. The more places you store stuff, the better the chance it will get lost.

Laptop considerations

Laptops are designed for portability, so keeping the number of cords and cables to a minimum is a must. The best digital camera accessories for a laptop are PCMCIA card adapters for your storage media. Just like a card reader, these adapters require no external power and download quickly and reliably. As shown in Figure D, they're small enough to carry around, even if you have several adapters to fit different media types.

Neat and tidy

There are worse problems in this world than having too many digital cameras, but keeping them organized will ensure that you can enjoy them to their fullest. It will also make it easier to find lesser-used accessories, such as software or filters, when you need them.

D

The PCMCIA card slot on a laptop computer gives you a fast download without the cords and cables.

Caring for your digital camera

Capturing a rainbow during a summer drizzle or a flowering cactus during a desert windstorm can be risky business when it comes to pulling out your digital camera to capture the shot. Digital cameras are much more expensive and sensitive than most traditional 35 mm cameras; therefore, you want to take steps to make them last. However, protecting your camera from the elements doesn't mean you have to miss incredible shots because of bad weather. It just means you need to take special precautions when doing so to ensure that your camera's 5,000th picture is as clear as the first!

Storing, traveling, and caring for your camera

When your digital camera is taking a break, it's important to store it correctly. Likewise, when you're on the go, you'll want to make sure it's well prepared for travel. Okay, so you're probably thinking to yourself that it doesn't take a nuclear physicist to pack and store a camera the right way, but just humor us! You may realize you've forgotten a simple step or you're neglecting other delicate accessories.

Have camera, will travel—or not!

Most of your picture taking will happen outside the confines of your own home. This means you need to make sure your camera is well protected for trips down the street or around the world. The care you put into packing your camera for a trip is the same care you should put into packing your camera for storage. The following are what you'll need to transport your camera correctly:

- **Purchase a camera bag or case.** This bag should fit not only your camera but your camera accessories as well. Don't use that old gym bag lying in your closet or that soft-sided cooler you use on picnics. We've seen this done and we don't recommend it. Make the investment in a functional and suitable case now and you'll be glad you did. With a good bag or case, you can pack your camera properly to ensure items stored in it won't bang against each other and cause damage.

- **Cover your lenses with lens caps or covers.** When storing and traveling with your camera, always make sure your lenses are protected. Since most digital cameras come with such equipment as batteries, straps, chargers, cables, and memory cards, you'll want to make sure the lenses are protected from these items. (Good packing also helps keep these additional components from becoming damaged.)

- **Store your camera in a safe location.** Make sure that this area is temperature controlled and clean. Avoid areas that are extremely cold or hot and dusty. It's also a good idea to remove your batteries before storing to prolong their life and minimize the risk of damage to your camera's battery contacts.

- **Be aware of strong magnetic fields.** If they are strong enough, magnetic fields can actually damage image data stored in the camera. To prevent this from happening, avoid storing your camera near electric motors and any other type of device that produces a strong magnetic field.

With the heightened security at airports, you may be worried that your stored digital images will get damaged when going through the metal detectors and X-ray machine. While this is certainly a valid concern, you have little to worry about. Current X-ray technology in the United States won't damage stored digital data. While it can "fog" traditional high-speed film, data stored on CompactFlash, SmartMedia, and other types of media isn't susceptible to the X-ray spectrum.

There is, however, a slight chance that the magnetic field produced by X-ray machines in foreign countries might damage your data. If you're in doubt, ask to have the media card hand-inspected. It might take a few extra minutes, but you can rest assured that your priceless images are safe.

Protect your camera from the elements

Extreme temperatures, sand, and water—sounds like a great ski trip or beach vacation for you, but it's no holiday for your camera. Every digital camera is different, but they all have many common predators, such as heat, extreme cold, sand, water (especially salt water), and more. The spaces around buttons and dials, as well as the many ports for various plug-ins, are perfect entry points for foreign objects. Because of this, you'll want to make sure you have your camera wrapped or in a case when you aren't using it—or just use a plastic zip-type bag. This will help keep all cracks and crevices free of debris. The following is a list of common dangers that you might encounter and how to prevent them from causing damage to your camera:

- **Extreme temperatures.** The camera, all lenses, and media should be kept away from excessive heat. If left in direct sunlight or in a hot car, the plastic components run the risk of melting and/or losing data. If your camera or storage device is exposed to extreme cold, allow it to acclimate to room temperature before operating. If you wish to take pictures in the cold environment, try to keep the camera in your coat, close to your body, when not in use.

You'll also want to avoid moving your camera from cold to warm locations because this causes condensation. When moisture from condensation collects behind your camera lens or the viewfinder, your picture quality may be affected. An inexpensive way to protect your camera from condensation is to simply seal it in a plastic bag immediately after you come in from the outdoors. Just keep it enclosed for an hour or so until it reaches room temperature.

- **Water.** As with all electronics, be careful around water. If you happen to get your digital camera wet or drop it in water, immediately turn the camera off and dry the outside with a cloth or towel. Let the camera completely dry out before trying to use it again. Most digital cameras, though not waterproof, will work after drying out, depending on the severity of the water exposure. If the camera is exposed to salt water, however, the chances of it working properly and not corroding are low.

- **Sand.** Sand can be very damaging. If you've ever tried to capture a great shot at the beach or in a desert when the wind was blowing, you might have heard a grinding sound when you tried to focus. If this happens it's a good idea to have your camera cleaned by a professional. Many camera manufacturers offer cleaning services, but if you're uncomfortable about sending your camera out to be cleaned, check with a local camera shop.

Take care of your batteries

The life of your batteries is directly related to how much you use your camera. They should remain charged for many images—unless, of course, you frequently use your flash or LCD panel, as the additional power required will run batteries down at a faster rate. But there's another danger when a battery is left in a digital camera. If you plan to store it for a long period of time, you should remove the batteries to avoid corrosion and a slow leeching of power. Even though your camera is turned off, a small amount of power can trickle out of the battery. Over time, you could have a problem on your hands.

When charging your battery, make sure you're using the correct adapter because using the wrong voltage adapter can ruin your battery and is a fire hazard. Also, converters can damage your batteries if used too frequently and for long periods of time. We recommend that you limit converter usage to a few hours at a time. Check your battery and the battery slot in your camera occasionally for condensation—keeping your battery dry will prevent corrosion.

Ensure the strength of your straps

Ensure that all straps are firmly connected. When hiking or climbing, it's a better idea to use a belt pack, since straps can get caught on branches or other objects and injure you (or your camera). Check the points where

Avoid damage to your tripod mount

Digital cameras are small, light, and portable, but these features can make them less durable. A problem that has occurred for many digital photographers with light, plastic-bodied digital cameras involves the tripod mount, which is commonly located on the bottom of the camera. When the tripod is screwed in too tightly, the mount can crack under the pressure and render it useless. If you have a plastic tripod mount on your digital camera, make sure you don't overtighten. Many camera manufacturers are switching to metal tripod mounts to make sure your digital camera can be safely secured to your tripod.

the strap attaches to the camera. If there are signs of wear, you should immediately switch straps or fix the existing one. Having your camera fall four feet to the ground as you're carrying it can cause catastrophic damage.

Keep your tripod level

Tripods are designed for quick setup and disassembly. However, this construction can make them susceptible to breakage. When setting up your tripod, ensure that there's a firm footing and that all clasps and turn bolts are secure before using it. Also, make sure that your camera is tightly connected to the tripod base before shooting. Not only will you get steadier images, but you'll also be able to use the tripod to its full potential. One last thing—make sure your camera's straps aren't wrapped around any of the tripod elements. A tangled strap can limit the operation of the tripod and make it more difficult to adjust. If you need to, use a piece of tape to hold the strap in a more convenient arrangement.

Keep track of your storage media

Taking care of your storage media is just common sense.

Memory Sticks, floppy disks, SmartMedia, CompactFlash, etc., all despise water, magnets, and heat. When your storage media is in your camera, you shouldn't have too many problems. Otherwise, make sure you have a safe place to keep your media, preferably in a location where it won't get damaged. You can find hard plastic cases for just about every type of media out there, either from an online digital photo site or from the manufacturer of the media. You can also find camera bags that have built-in storage for digital media. With the price of storage still relatively high, protecting this investment makes sense.

Stay ever vigilant!

The most important bit of advice when it comes to caring for your digital camera and its accessories is to always be on guard. While getting that once-in-a-lifetime shot of a surfer riding the waves during a hurricane may be worth it, weigh the pros and cons of having to replace your camera after the salt, sand, and water destroy the mechanisms of your delicate camera. Be prepared— have a good bag along with good handling and storage techniques and your camera will last for many years.

Cleaning your camera's lens

Fingerprints, smudges, dirt, dust, water drops, and scratches—they all plot against you! When trying to take the best possible quality images with your digital camera, any of these contaminants can mess up your lens and prevent you from getting the crystal-clear pictures it was designed to capture. Having a strategy for avoiding a dirty lens is just as important as knowing how to properly clean it. Not only will caring for your lens produce better, more consistently sharp images, but it will also extend the life of your optics and allow you to get more from your digital dollar.

A

One way to protect your lens is to add a filter over the lens, such as this UV filter added to an Nikon digital camera.

The importance of a clean lens

Your lens is designed to produce clear, sharp images using precision optics and high-tech lens coatings. When the lens gets dirty, your image quality degrades. Smudges, fingerprints, dirt, and haze on your lens reduce image contrast, introduce lens flare, and can cause hazy, out-of-focus pictures. Not cleaning a dirty lens can also hit you in the pocketbook—if you don't take care of your optics, there will come a point where your image quality suffers so much you might have to replace the lens. And with only a few digital cameras with removable lenses on the market, it's more likely you'll have to replace the entire digital camera. Taking the time to care for your camera's lens will not only help produce the best quality images, but it will also

ensure that your investment in a digital camera continues to pay off.

Keep your mitts off your lens

The best way to care for a lens is to never have to clean it in the first place. The lens of a digital camera has complex lens coatings that reduce glare, manage ultraviolet rays, and perform other valuable image-improving functions. Every time you clean your lens, you run the risk of damaging these coatings. However, it's practically impossible to avoid the lens entirely, and inevitably the lens will get dirty. But there are a few ways you can minimize the time between cleanings.

Keep it in the bag

The best defense against the world of fingerprints and dust is keeping your camera's lens cover on when the camera isn't in use. Your camera probably came with

Cleaning your optical viewfinder

As time goes on and you use your digital camera more, it's inevitable that a bit of dirt and dust will get into the optical viewfinder area. Since these spaces are commonly recessed, it's easy for debris to get lodged in the tight space, possibly obscuring your view, but definitely looking a bit nasty. To tidy up the viewfinder itself:

1. Mix a small batch of window cleaning fluid and water together in equal amounts. Since the optical viewfinder is most likely uncoated plastic, any household glass cleaner will do the job, but if you're in doubt, consult your camera's manual for specific cleaning instructions.

2. Lightly moisten a cotton swab with the fluid and then gently clean the surface of the viewerfinder. Don't push too hard or excess fluid could seep in and cause clouding within the viewfinder. Also, try to avoid getting the fluid on the rubberized portions of the viewfinder, as this can cause this material to dry out.

3. Use the dry end of the cotton swab to lightly wipe the viewfinder.

a small string or elastic band to attach your lens cap to your camera, as it's easy to lose the cap otherwise. If you don't have a camera lens cover strap or a lens cover, your local camera shop should carry them. For even greater protection, when not in use, keep the camera in a camera bag to further insulate it from the world of contaminates.

Use proper handling

Another way to avoid getting the lens dirty is to hold the camera properly. The diminutive size of digital cameras has made it easier to grab your digital camera by the fistful, but this can lead to fingerprints and smudges on your lens. Make sure you steer your fingers clear of the lens and handle the camera with care when removing it from a pocket or camera bag.

If your digital camera has the ability to accommodate add-on lenses, you might want to think about adding a UV filter to your lens, as shown in **Figure A** on the previous page. A UV filter adds a layer of protection to your more-expensive glass while blocking the UV spectrum. Plus, if your UV filter gets scratched, it will cost you around $15 to replace it rather than hundreds of dollars for a new camera or lens.

The best lens-cleaning equipment

There are plenty of options on the market for cleaning your lens, but many of them are so specialized it can be confusing to determine the best method. As we mentioned earlier, any

lens-cleaning method has its pros and cons, so keeping your technique simple is the best approach. There are two stages to cleaning a lens: removing particulate matter and then cleaning the surface of the lens. Let's take a look at what equipment is available to get these jobs done.

Dust in the wind

The first step to take when cleaning a lens is to remove the larger particles, such as dust and dirt, that might scratch the lens. These particles are usually big enough to simply blow off, which is good for the lens. Anytime you can clean the lens without actually touching it, you reduce the possibility of damaging it. While you can buy specialized dust blowers from your local camera store, most photographers use a standard ear syringe, which you can buy inexpensively from your local drugstore. This device pushes out a focused, but gentle, puff of air that you can easily control.

You may be asking: Why not just blow on it? Well, when you use your breath to clean your lens, you bring moisture into the equation (more on that later). It's important to avoid putting moisture directly on the lens, as it can work its way inside the lens and cause fogging. For the same reason, using cans of pressurized air can be troublesome if used inappropriately. While they can be very effective, there's the chance that the highly pressurized air will condense upon exit from the canister and shoot out a blast of freezing-cold water. And if there's one thing a lens hates more than water, it's cold water, which can cause cracking and warping of the lens housing.

Another option for removing particulate matter is the use of a soft bristled brush, such as an artist's sable brush. These can be very effective when trying to remove stubborn dust particles, but beware of embedded debris in the bristles, as they can drag across the surface of your lens and scratch it. If you're using a brush, make sure to keep it clean and avoid touching the bristles, which can pick up the natural oils from your hands.

(Not) scratching the surface
Once the loose dust and dirt are removed, you can clean the surface of the lens, if necessary. Nine times out of 10, removing the dust on the lens is all you'll need, but if you have oily smudges and fingerprints on the lens, you'll have to remove them. There are wet or dry approaches. Each type of cleaning works well; it really depends on where your preference lies.

High and dry
Don't just grab any dry cloth and start wiping your lens. Using the edge of your shirt or a napkin at the dinner table can cause some serious damage to your lens surface. You never know what lurks in these types of material, so it's best to use a dry cloth specially made to clean lenses. Several manufacturers produce microfiber cloths made

up of infinitesimal nooks and crannies that remove debris from the surface of the lens. These synthetic cloths are washable and reusable, so keeping one in your camera kit is a necessity. You can also purchase packs of disposable lens tissues that can perform the same duties in a pinch. Check out your local camera store for these types of lens-cleaning cloths—they'll probably have a variety of options to choose from.

Wet and wild
There are many types of lens-cleaning fluids on the market. We can't tell you which one is better than another; they're all quite similar. Just remember to never pour lens-cleaning fluid directly on your lens. As we mentioned earlier, excess fluid can sneak under the lens housing and cause major problems. Always apply your cleaning fluid to a microfiber cloth or lens tissue, and then lightly wipe the surface of your lens in a circular motion. Make sure each swipe is made with a clean part of the cloth and finish the job by taking one last wipe with a dry portion.

You can also buy a "lens pen," which is basically a two-sided cleaning tool. One side of the pen contains a soft-bristle brush for removing dirt and dust, while the other side contains a cleaning pad soaked in cleaning fluid. Some people swear by lens pens, some people hate them, but at less than $10 each, it might not be a bad thing to have in your camera bag.

Taking your digital camera to the beach
If you plan to take your digital camera to the beach or spend anytime taking digital images in hot weather, there are some steps you can take to protect the delicate electronics and optics from the heat of summer:

- Always avoid leaving your digital camera in direct sunlight, as the intense heat can melt adhesives in the camera body. Use a light-colored shirt or towel to cover your camera, and try not to store your camera in a closed car, where temperatures easily reach 120 degrees on a hot day.

- Keep your camera protected from sand and water damage by placing it in a camera bag or plastic zip-type bag when not in use.

- Don't place your digital camera in a cooler with ice in it. While doing so seems to make sense, there's a high risk that potentially damaging condensation will develop once the camera is moved to the warmer air.

Part 2—Shooting Techniques

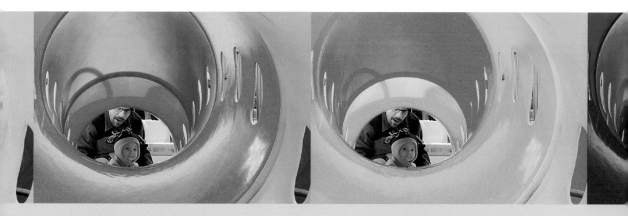

While digital photography provides the advantage of instantly reviewing your photos, you'll still benefit from perfecting your shooting techniques. Taking the time to learn and practice some tricks of the trade will help you to produce better images more quickly. In this part, we'll introduce you to techniques for taking pictures of children and pets, as well as memorable photographs of special events. We'll also show you how to take great shots outdoors and in specialty lighting situations. We'll discuss ways that you can improve image quality before you take each shot, and finally, we'll go over technical tips that will help to make your pictures the best they can be.

Photographing kids and pets

Whether you're a professional photographer, an advanced amateur, or just a proud family member recording a special moment for the future, taking pictures of children is one of the most rewarding things a photographer can do. It's been said that you can't take a bad picture of a child, and due to the wide range of emotions and expressions that a child can exhibit, most people would agree.

What about family pets? Many people would apply the exact same statement to them, since many of us consider our dog or cat to be another member of the family. Trying to capture these moments can be a little tricky, though, since your subject may not always want to sit still for you!

Your subjects: Will they ever stop moving?

When you start to photograph children and pets, you quickly learn one of the biggest drawbacks is that they won't hold still. Children often have short attention spans, and your dog or cat may have an even shorter one. Generally, having a favorite toy handy can be helpful, as it will hold the child's or animal's attention long enough to snap some pictures. One of the best methods to get the picture you want isn't the most obvious: Put your camera

down for a few minutes and take a little time to play with your subjects; talk to them if necessary.

Essential tools for the shoot

One of the biggest (and most expensive) items we can recommend is a larger memory card. Most digital cameras come with an 8 MB or 16 MB card. When shooting at a higher resolution, you'll probably fill up these cards quickly. When we've used a 1 GB card in the camera and the higher resolutions, we could store between 500 and 700 images. Having this kind of space allows you to continue shooting uninterrupted, which will result in more captured moments.

Using a flash

One of the first things to be aware of is the use of the flash in your images. In some cases, flash is necessary, but usually using a flash is just a matter of individual preference. Here are some ideas on how to make the decision.

Seeing the light when it comes to using a flash

Figures A and B show photographs of our first model, Allison, which we took using flash and natural light, respectively. As you can

A

In this photo, we captured Allison with the on-camera flash filling in the shadows.

B

Allison is posing sweetly in this photo, which we took using the available natural light.

see, both methods capture a beautiful moment, each with its own subtle difference in texture and mood. In this case, the use of flash would be an individual preference. By keeping the aperture at f/2 to f/2.8 and focusing on the eyes, you'll get photos that are picture perfect.

Even though the flash image shown in **Figure A** is brighter and has captured more detail than the naturally lit image shown in **Figure B**, it appears more stark in comparison. Most digital cameras do a good job of balancing the flash with natural light, as shown in our pictures of Allison. Natural light, however, has a beautiful quality of its own. Try it both ways to see what works best for you.

Note: *Try to maintain eye contact with your subject. When the eyes look right into the lens and you snap the shot, you're guaranteed a good result.*

Capturing subjects that often fly by in a flash

Jeff the cat was an interesting subject to photograph. You'll need to be patient, quick … and forget about the posed part when photographing animals.

While Jeff, seen hunting in **Figure C**, went about stalking his prey, we couldn't get a crisp shot of him using the natural light. As you can see, there's a bit of a gray and unfocused cast to the image.

Remember when we said there would be instances where you'd need flash? Well, this is one of them. Flash is necessary with moving subjects. Our on-camera flash came in handy

C
Jeff the cat goes into stalk mode, which makes getting a sharp and simple natural light shot difficult.

D
Jeff was still stalking, but using our on-camera flash, we were able to get a sharp shot of him.

here because it enabled us to record the details of our subject while he continued to hunt. As you can see in **Figure D**, the resulting image is quite acceptable.

A return to an old classic: Black and white images

One of the best functions on most digital cameras is the black and white function. Although black and white photography has declined in popularity over the years, it's

back with a vengeance. But this time, with digital cameras, there are no messy chemicals or expensive darkrooms, only the beauty of an image that looks unique when compared to color photography.

As you can see in **Figure E** on the next page, black and white images have an editorial, almost old-fashioned feel to them. These images can be further enhanced in most image-editing programs, and different toning effects (such as sepia toning) can make them seem even more like family heirlooms.

Combining kids and pets in the same shot

When it comes to putting children and pets together for a photo opportunity, you need to be ready to take quite a few snapshots to get the desired image you're looking for. We decided to photograph Emily with two of her pets. First was her cat, Dewey, who wasn't in the mood to be photographed that day. Emily herself had been in better moods as well, and things were looking a little grim. However, when they started rolling on the ground, the mood seemed to change for the better, as you can see in **Figure F**. We kept the shutter speed to 1/250 of a second to better capture the spontaneity of the moment.

Emily's other pet definitely won't be for everyone, but as a photographic subject, it couldn't be beat. Jessica is an albino Burmese python—tame, gentle, but quite a handful when she's out. It isn't often you get a chance to photograph a child who's comfortable around such a creature. When photographing exotic pets, you'll find it pays to have someone around (like a parent, handler, or owner) who can handle the animal while you shoot.

In our case, Jessica turned out to be quite a brilliant subject. Her yellow markings set her off nicely against the green color of the grass. The only issue was getting all 10 feet of Jessica in the frame along with Emily. Using the camera lens at the widest setting allowed us to frame Jessica and Emily together. A square crop with the snake running along the edges and Emily in the upper-right corner, as shown in **Figure G**, solved that issue as well. We set the aperture to f/5.6 (to allow us to get both subjects in focus) and the camera shutter speed to 1/100 of a second.

Off to the beach!

Our second location, the beach, gave the kids we were photographing a new place to play and gave us a new place to take pictures. We spent some

E

The absence of color in this shot of Andrew (appearing a little more angelic in black and white) is a great way to draw attention to your subject's softer side.

F

Emily and Dewey share a special moment—unplanned and unposed.

G

Emily and her 10-foot friend look cute and comfortable with each other on the grass.

time experimenting with the camera, following the kids with it set to a slower shutter speed, as shown in **Figure H**. A shutter speed of 1/20 or lower gives the effect shown; just try to keep up with the kids!

The slower shutter speed blurs the image. However, if you follow your subject closely, a portion of the image will remain in focus. This gives the feeling of motion. Fun images of the children clowning around for the camera can be a real treasure, like the one we took of Emily, shown in **Figure I**. Setting the camera at its widest lens setting, turning the macro focus option on, and getting in tight can result in some images that emphasize the whimsical nature of children.

H

If you follow your subject with a slower shutter speed, it results in dynamic images like the one shown here.

I

The combination of the wide-angle lens and the position of the railing make for a fun photograph.

Keeping your subjects' attention

We've collected some tried-and-true techniques you can use to get kids and pets to pay attention during a photo shoot:

- A good way to keep the attention of children is to get down and play with them while you take their photograph. Talking to kids as you take their picture is another good way to keep their attention. Babies and small children also respond well to having Mom or Dad in close range. Providing your young charges with variety is another good (and fun!) way to keep their attention.

One way to do this is to have fun props on hand, such as a toy frog, crown, and magic wand for a little princess or art supplies and an easel for the aspiring artist. You can also arrange to photograph them at different locations such as the beach, the zoo, or perhaps even the local planetarium.

- In place of the spoken commands that work for well-trained pets, be creative with animals. A treat or bright toy just next to or behind the focal point of the camera works quite well. When pho-

tographing our own pets, we've used bounce flash or fill flash on most occasions and the animals hardly bat an eye.

- It's important to be flexible at times. Keep in mind that you may need to alter a setup.

- Avoid skimping on the number of shots you take. This way, you're sure to wind up with one or more agreeable images. Beyond that, imagination, compassion, and a little old-fashioned ingenuity go a long way.

Candid photography techniques

While some of the best candid pictures are taken by simply pointing the camera and pressing the shutter button, most are the result of a unique mix of spontaneity and technique. The informal nature of candid photography requires that you be aware of your surroundings and prepared to react when that special moment arises. You must also develop the ability to blend into your environment, allowing your subjects to go about their activities naturally. By being mindful of some simple photographic techniques and utilizing the best features of your digital camera, you can put yourself in position to capture great candid shots while still having fun.

Evaluate the scene

It's important to understand your subjects, their activities, and how they fit into their environment before you start shooting. However, it's even more important to understand what you'll need to do to get a good shot, such as:

- Make sure you have a good feel for the available light in your scene. Using the flash should be avoided when capturing a candid moment, as it not only gives you away, but it also only gives you one shot to get it right.

- Think about how you're going to frame your shot. Look for shooting positions that maximize your subject by eliminating distracting backgrounds.

- Consider using the zoom feature on your digital camera to not only place yourself inconspicuously away from your subject, but also to reduce your depth of field, further separating your subject from background elements. In **Figure A**, we eliminated the distracting bright windows by shooting down on

A

When shooting candid shots, make sure the background doesn't distract from your subject. If it does, reframe your shot to improve it.

the subject. The result is a better-framed shot with the subject clearly emphasized.

- Candid photography relies on catching your subject off-guard, so do your best to blend into your surroundings. If you take the time to evaluate your scene, you'll be able to choose your spots to keep your presence discreet.

Get your camera ready

Your shooting situations dictate the settings on your camera, but here are a few suggestions that work in most of them:

- Candid shots require speed; shoot at a higher ISO so your camera can select a faster shutter speed. Since blurriness can be a problem when your lens is in a telephoto position, a fast shutter speed also helps freeze any movement and helps make up for any unsteadiness.

- Try to pre-focus your shot to eliminate any lag caused by autofocus. This isn't always practical, but if you have a good idea of where your subject is going to be positioned, you can shave off precious milliseconds from your exposure.

- Avoid a center-weighted mode if you're using autofocus and shooting more than one subject, as your digital camera might focus on the space in between your subjects instead. **Figure B** shows a great scene thwarted by

B

While this scene provided a great candid moment, active focus mode got in the way of a good shot. Be aware of the pitfalls of active focus mode and reduce problems by pre-focusing.

a center-weighted focus mode. Go with a zone or matrix focusing option, if available, and you can avoid blurry shots.

Be ready to shoot

When the moment arises, shoot away. Take as many shots as you can before your subject is on to you. If your digital camera has a pronounced shutter delay, adjust when you press the shutter button to compensate. If you miss a shot, don't worry. Just be patient and continue to observe your subject. If the person is on to you, disappear for a few minutes and re-evaluate your shooting opportunities.

The digital advantage

Digital cameras have a few advantages that can help you record candid moments:

- Since they don't use film, there's no audible film advance noise. And unless

you're using a professional digital SLR, the shutter noise should be minimal from a digital camera.

- If you use a large capacity memory card, digital cameras give you the freedom to take many shots without having to change a roll of film or worry about processing fees.

- Some digital cameras have rotating LCD screens for viewing, so use it to your advantage. Not only does it allow you to frame a shot without bringing the camera to your eye level, but it can allow you to get unique perspectives by shooting from a range of low and high angles.

- Most digital cameras are small in size, allowing the photographer to hide them until the last minute. This allows you to catch your subjects behaving naturally before they have time to strike a still pose.

Creating great holiday pictures

One of the busiest times of the year for any camera is the holiday season, when everyone comes together for celebrations, occasions, and parties. With the convenience and capabilities of digital cameras at your side, you can capture the holiday revelry and create some lasting memories through your photography.

The challenges of holiday shots

Holiday shots run the photographic gamut. There are low-light situations, group shots, individual shots, outdoor shots, close-ups, portraits, bright colors, harsh reflections—the list of photographic challenges goes on and on. The varied landscape of holiday photography requires you to be flexible, understand your digital camera's capabilities, and use your shooting environment to get the best possible shots. So, while holiday shots aren't hard to take, taking the time to plan your shots and prepare your camera will help you overcome these photographic obstacles.

Prepare your hardware

Digital cameras are small, versatile, and easy to use, which makes them perfect for crowded holiday gatherings. To get the best pictures once you arrive, take some time to prepare your camera before you get there.

Plenty of power, plenty of memory

First and most important, charge up those batteries and keep a spare set handy. You don't want to miss Uncle Lou sleeping on the couch after dinner, do you? Next, give your memory cards a good "cleaning." Using your camera or card reader, reformat your card to maximize the capacity and remove any old files or folders that might be taking up space. Reformatting has the added benefit of giving your digital camera a clean slate, which decreases the time you have to wait while a picture is saving.

Auto white balance

Incandescent setting

A
By evaluating the dominant light source in this scene, we were able to adjust the camera to a white balance setting that matched the environment.

Clean up your act

You should also make sure you clean your camera's lens. Remove any smudges or specks of dirt that can spoil a batch of great photos. Make sure you use a good lens cloth, lens brush, or cleaning fluid designed for camera optics. Avoid the temptation to use something like a paper towel, as it can cause permanent damage to your lens. Bring your camera, your external flash (if you have that capability), and perhaps a wide-angle lens. Keep it simple and bring only what you're going to use—you'll have more fun and increase your chances of actually being where the action is.

Educate yourself

Finally, take a few minutes to flip through your camera manual. Make sure you understand how to adjust the exposure levels and look for special scene modes that might benefit your situation. Many digital cameras have a Party or Indoors scene setting that will optimize the exposure settings to fit the environment.

Arriving at the party

The best holiday photos are candid, so stopping to adjust your camera settings before a shot can spoil the moment. Get your camera ready to anticipate the shooting environment—then you can click away without worry.

Make a resolution

Your first decision is to choose the quality and resolution settings for your camera. We're firm believers that you should always shoot at the highest resolution possible, but this increases memory consumption and the time it takes to save your files to the memory card. Lower resolution settings save quickly and take up less room, but they aren't as detailed and can look pixelated when printed. Try to find a happy medium that maximizes the capabilities of your camera, your storage size, and your shooting style.

I'm dreaming of a white balance

Next, take a look around you. What type of light is dominant? If the holiday party is during the day and natural light is everywhere, you'll want to set your white balance for a daylight setting. However, during the winter holidays you're likely to be indoors under incandescent or fluorescent light. Adjust your white balance accordingly and you'll save yourself from having to adjust the images later. If you aren't sure what to choose or if you have a mixed-light situation, select the automatic white balance setting and let the camera do the work for you. **Figure A** shows how a proper white balance setting can produce more accurate colors and a better-looking image.

Flash considerations

Another big variable is which flash setting to use. An external flash is really the best option, but if you don't have this capability, think about your flash range and how it will affect your image. The built-in flashes on most digital cameras are extremely bright, so keep some distance from your subject to allow the light to diffuse. Otherwise, you could get hotspots and harsh shadows. Back up and use your camera's zoom lens to compensate, and you'll get more evenly lit scenes. As shown in **Figure B**, in some cases, turning the flash off can produce images that capture the mood of the holiday much better.

Another issue with the flash is the dreaded red eye. If you plan to concentrate on shots of people, seriously consider using the red eye reduction mode on your camera. A brightly lit room will make your subjects' pupils smaller and reduce the chance for reflected light from the retina.

Note: Another technique that's easy (if you have the equipment) and natural looking is to use professional strobe heads for lighting your shots. Instead of using them as a direct light (very unflattering) or using light modifiers, such as soft boxes and umbrellas (too cumbersome), try taking the strobe heads and bouncing the lights directly off the ceiling.

Exposure settings

Finally, let's quickly discuss ISO settings. Holiday parties are usually slow-moving affairs, so shoot at ISO 100 or ISO 200. Higher ISO settings invite noise to the party, so keep your images as clean as possible with a low ISO. If the party moves outside for sledding, change to a higher shutter speed, but change it back once you head inside for hot chocolate. Once you've set your camera, take some test shots and preview them on your LCD. If you see problems, adjust your settings before the rest of the guests arrive.

Getting down to business

Of course, you'll have to ask people to pose now and again, but try to capture natural shots of people talking and laughing. A good photographer blends into the background and captures people in a more relaxed mood.

Think about the details that make the holiday special and try to capture them in your pictures. Lights, candles, special foods and desserts, wreaths,

and the like can help tell the whole story of an event. Don't be afraid to get close and record smaller details like ornaments or bows—anything that defines the moment is fair game, as shown in **Figures C** and **D**.

Simplicity is best

When framing your shot, try to keep your subject centrally located and avoid clutter in the background. Use your camera's LCD panel to preview your shot, and explore different perspectives to remove any unwanted details in the background or you might end up with cluttered images. Shoot horizontally as well as vertically to best fit your subject matter. By simplifying the shot, you'll end up with a stronger image.

Anticipate the shot

While some of the best shots are spontaneous, anticipating a moment is a skill that can be developed. Be ready when a child is opening a gift to capture the look on her face. If you're waiting for the punch line to a joke, focus in on a jovial relative and capture his laughter. In

B

The first shot is overwhelmed by the bright flash, while the second shot uses the ambient light to create a better representation of the occasion.

essence, be ready. You never know what's going to happen.

Group shots

With the whole family together, it's time for a group shot. However, most people find setting up a group shot to be boring, so try to plan your group shots all at once. Get everyone together before sitting down to eat. That way, everyone will be motivated by food and behave for you. You'll also be able to set them up, knock 'em down, and send everyone to the table for some good eats.

Sharing your photos

One of the benefits of digital cameras is the ability to instantly share your images with the partygoers. Instead of using your tiny LCD panel to share, however, bring your video cable along to display your pictures on the television. Then, the whole crowd can see your shots. Unfortunately, your vertical images might display horizontally onscreen, but if you don't have too many of them, your friends and family will forgive you.

Note: *When shooting holiday parties, give up the role of photographer every now and again and get some shots of yourself. If you want to maintain control, use the camera's self-timer feature or the remote control, if available, to get yourself in the shots.*

Is that a tree growing out of her head?

When framing casual portraits, make sure there isn't anything growing out of your subject's head. Tree limbs, signs, flowers, window frames—these are just a few of many items that can distract from the strength of your image. When framing your image, check your viewfinder or LCD preview to see if any objects are popping out where they shouldn't be. If necessary, move your subject in front of a simple, neutral background that will emphasize the foreground, not the background.

C

Photographing detailed images, such as this individual place setting, record special touches at a particular event.

D

Grabbing a few shots of the food before everyone digs in helps preserve the memories of the dishes served.

Photographing sunsets

There's something about a sunset that makes you want to reach for your camera. Perhaps it's the wide range of warm colors and tones, the dramatic silhouettes of clouds and objects, or the serenity of the slowly fading sun. A photograph of a sunset defines a unique moment that only existed as that image was captured. While many sunset pictures may look similar, no two are exactly alike. But there are a few tricks to make sure your sunset shots come out stunning and not so cliché. These tricks will also help you respond to some of the unique challenges faced when shooting a sunset with a digital camera.

The science of sunsets

While you don't want to encourage pollution in the air, understanding your location and atmospheric conditions can help you determine if this evening's sunset is going to be a rare display. A good sunset may pop up under any circumstance, but if you can find a hot, humid night with low wind and a location that's close to a city or desert (dust from the sand does a great job scattering light), you have the best chance to get a great shot.

Composing your shot

Arriving a half hour or so before the show starts gives you enough time to take full advantage of the sun's rays as they change from minute to minute. Of course, a tripod helps you maintain your framing and keep your shot steady.

Finding the right spot

When selecting a location from which to shoot, keep in mind that your hero in this shot is the sunset, not other elements in the scene. For that reason, position yourself to allow an unrestricted view of the sun. This may be a beach, a cliff's edge, or the shoreline of a lake—the important thing is that your view of the sky isn't obstructed, as shown in **Figure A**. If this isn't an option, position yourself so you can see the maximum amount of the horizon and reduce the prominence of distracting elements.

A

Keeping your horizon line uncluttered emphasizes the sun and the sky.

Setting the scene

Follow the Rule of Thirds in this situation—keep the horizon level low and fill your shot with the sky. Keeping some of the darker foreground in your shot helps emphasize the sky, adds greater interest, and sets the scene for your shot. Consider adding other elements, such as birds, trees, etc., to your shot, creating interesting silhouetted figures. Of course, most great sunset shots include a cloud or two, so if you're lucky enough to have some low clouds, use them to your benefit, as in the shot shown in **Figure B**.

B

In this shot, low clouds contrast against the saturated colors in the sky.

Note: *When preparing your shot, avoid looking directly at the sun, whether with the naked eye or through your viewfinder. This can cause serious eye injury. Using your digital camera's LCD panel to frame your shot is much safer and usually gives you more accurate framing.*

Prepping your digital camera settings

Sunsets are typically a low-light situation. While dealing with low-light levels with digital cameras is challenging enough, you're up against a steady decline of available light as the sun fades away. Your exposure settings and your image sensor's sensitivity to light (ISO) are your best defense in these varying light conditions, but there are other factors to consider as well. Next, we'll show you how to use your digital camera's settings to conquer these challenges.

Making the most out of low light

Many digital cameras have exposure compensation, but most don't come near the range of settings available on a traditional SLR camera. So, metering your sunset is certainly the most professional way to shoot, but perhaps not the most practical, considering the limitations of current digital setups. Plus, to get the most accurate reading, you'd have to meter every few minutes as the sun sinks toward the horizon. For these reasons, we recommend using your camera's internal light meter to evaluate the scene, then bracketing up and down one stop.

Note: *Underexposing your shots slightly often makes the colors in your scene richer.*

The next consideration in low-light situations is setting your image sensor's sensitivity to light, achieved by adjusting your camera's ISO settings. Keep these settings low (ISO 100 and 200), as higher ISO settings can encourage pixelated noise in your image. While setting your ISO low makes the shutter stay open longer, the visible noise in the shot will be greatly reduced by the less-sensitive image sensor.

Other camera settings

Since your subject isn't anywhere near you and really isn't going anywhere fast, it's a good idea to set your focus to a center-weighted setting.

If you have the ability to set focus, set it to infinity to keep the sun and horizon line in focus. Don't worry about your foreground objects; they'll just be silhouettes anyway. If you have an autofocus camera, it's most likely to select Infinity anyway, so don't worry too much about it.

While the clarity of your foreground subjects isn't that important, keeping them silhouetted against the background is essential. So turn off your flash already!

Timing is everything

Now that you've set your camera and framed your shot, it's time to shoot. Hopefully, you've loaded up your highest capacity memory card because the best technique is to click away. The light in the sky and your natural elements, such as clouds and water, are going to change rapidly during the sunset, so continue to fire that shutter. Keep in mind that many of the best sunset shots don't even include the sun, so stick around a few minutes once it slips below the horizon and the sky begins to glow, as shown in **Figure C.**

C

A good sunset image doesn't always feature the sun.

Nighttime photography

As the day turns to night, the rods in your eyes take over as you try to see in the low light. While the cones provide your brain with most of the color information, the rods show the world in grayscale, with only subtle hints of color. Unlike your eyes, an image sensor doesn't have rods and cones, so it still sees the world in color, even in low light. While there may not be much light available, taking long exposures of a scene allows light to build up and reveal a colorful nighttime world. To capture great low-light shots, you need to take some steps to make sure your images don't end up dark and blurry.

After the sun goes down

When photographers talk about night photography, they aren't talking about shooting without light. Light must reach the image sensor for an image to be produced, so having a light source is an absolute necessity. However, this light doesn't have to be very bright, as long as it's somewhat predictable.

For example, the low-light photographer's best friend is the moon. On a clear night when the moon is rising, the full moon is usually bright enough to light almost any scene, provided you use a long enough exposure.

We use the term *low-light* photography here because calling it simply *night* photography can be misleading. This is because some of the best shots are taken in the hour or so after sunset, when the light of the sky is fairly bright and relatively even, as shown in **Figure A**. For the best natural light, shooting when the moon is rising or soon before or after dusk are your best bets for getting good color and detail in your low-light shots.

Tip: You can capture great nighttime shots after a rain, when the slick surfaces reflect light in unexpected places.

Digital and darkness

Digital cameras still have a way to go when it comes to shooting in low-light settings, mostly because the shutter must remain open longer to let in enough light to form the image. When the shutter is open, the pixels on the image sensor receiving the light tend to heat up, which can cause thermal noise. It appears in your image as off-color or white "spots," the result of a toasty pixel (or two or three) misreading the information, as shown in **Figure B**.

A
Low light doesn't mean no light. Some of the best shots are taken right after the sun goes down.

B
In this enlargement, you can see that a considerable amount of noise developed in this long (90-second) exposure.

How do you avoid this? There are a few techniques for keeping your pixels cool and comfortable. First, nighttime is usually cooler, so it takes longer for pixels to warm up. Shooting in colder winter weather extends this time even more. The shot shown in **Figure C**, which was taken in sub-freezing weather, took much longer to develop noise. The image shown in **Figure B** was taken at 65 degrees, so the sensor heated up more quickly. Second, take your longer exposures as soon as you turn your camera on. If you have to take consecutive shots, turn the camera off and give it a chance to chill out before you start another exposure. Finally, set your camera's ISO setting for ISO 100, or the lowest you can get. Higher ISO settings increase the sensitivity of your image sensor and can lead to a fast buildup of noise.

What to bring to the shoot

A nighttime shoot is a little different than taking snapshots

at the company picnic. First, forget about handholding your camera. The steadier the surface you provide during the longer exposures, the less likely your shots will be blurry from camera movement. The slightest shake can ruin a 30-second exposure, so make sure you have a tripod or some other stabilizing device like a beanbag to keep your camera steady.

For the same reason, you'll want to reduce your contact with the camera as much as possible. Even pressing the shutter button can cause movements that can show up in your shot, so use other ways of activating the shutter, if possible. If your camera has a remote control, by all means use it (but make sure the infrared beam doesn't show up in your shot). If you don't have a remote control, check to see if your camera can use a manual cable release so you don't have to touch the camera directly. This device also allows you to manually control the length of time the shutter is open. If neither of these is an option, go for the old standby— the self-timer.

C

Believe it or not, the only available light in this scene was a crescent moon. The cold temperature helped reduce the development of thermal noise during the long exposure.

Setting your digital camera

There are many different digital cameras out there with a wide range of features and capabilities, so we'll present a number of suggested settings you can apply to your own digital camera. While some simpler digital cameras are poorly suited to low-light shooting, you can get a good shot from most models, provided you choose your settings wisely.

Exposing yourself

Low-light photography demands long exposures, so you need to keep the shutter open as long as possible. Some cameras may top out at a couple of seconds, so check your camera's manual and see what yours can do. If your camera has a Bulb (B) mode, you have the ability to keep the shutter open as long as you like, which is preferable for low-light photography. Make sure you understand how the shutter is opened and closed—do you need to click once to open it and once to close it, or do you have to hold down the button during the entire exposure? Remember, stability is key during long exposures, so go for the option that keeps the camera the steadiest.

The length of your exposure depends on the amount of available light and the effect you're trying to achieve. Since you can't meter the scene accurately, deciding on an exposure time is largely trial and error. Start with a few-second exposure and work your way up. Check your images on the LCD as you shoot, and you can quickly see if you have a good image. As shown in **Figure D**, we started with a 1-second exposure and kept experimenting until we got the exposure we were looking for.

Shutter speed is really the key to good low-light shots, but you can also use your aperture setting. Most consumer-level

or semi-professional digital cameras allow you to set an aperture priority or shutter priority with the camera deciding the rest. If you have a fully manual digital camera, experiment with using your largest aperture, which lets in more light. However, keep in mind that larger apertures decrease your depth of field, so if you're shooting for details, you may want to use a smaller setting.

Coming into focus

Using autofocus in low light can be problematic, as your camera has less detail to focus in on than it would in daylight (or artificial light). Using a fully automatic matrix metering autofocus may befuddle your digital camera's brain. Our recommendation is to use a spot meter mode, where the camera measures in the center of the frame only. This technique works well when you have a background that's very dark or very light. If your subject is off center, check for an area spot focus mode that lets you designate which portion of the frame should be measured.

***

Note: *You can also set your camera to focus on infinity, especially if you're photographing a subject that doesn't have distinct objects in the foreground.*

***

Adding some flash

Using a flash at night is only useful if you want to add light to a foreground object and then expose for the background,

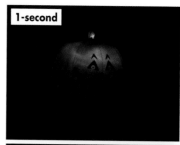

D

By starting with a relatively short (1-second) exposure, we were able to make an intelligent guess on how much longer we needed to get a good image. Try different time intervals until you find the one that gives you the best shot.

as shown in **Figure E**. When shooting at night, it's best just to turn off the flash.

Using other options

There are a few more options to be aware of when shooting in low light. Whether it's worth setting a white balance is up for debate, but some photographers suggest selecting a daylight/sunlight setting when shooting at night. Huh? Well, a daylight/sunlight setting is designed to emphasize the warmer tones in the scene, which could help heat up your cooler nighttime colors. Speaking of scenes, your camera may have a Scene mode designed to optimize the camera for nighttime shooting. Look for a setting named Night, Night Portrait, or even an Indoors setting and try a couple of shots. Finally, you can increase the sensitivity of your image sensor by increasing the exposure compensation. This may let in more light, but it's a double-edged sword. A more sensitive sensor is more likely to develop thermal noise, while a less sensitive sensor needs a longer exposure time, which in turn may also cause the development of noise.

The key to success

One of the benefits of digital photography is that you can view your image immediately on the LCD screen after capture and make adjustments while still onsite. You can also take shots without worrying about processing and printing charges, so you can feel free to take some risks and try out some new techniques. You also have a record of the exposure settings recorded along with the image. The EXIF data saved with your image records the exposure time, aperture, and a wealth of other information. When you view an image that looks great, note what combination of settings made it what it is.

E

If you're trying to capture details in objects that are close to the camera, such as this tree, you can try your camera's flash. When shooting at night, however, turning it off is usually the best practice.

Photographing autumn colors

Autumn is the time of year when almost everything you look at begs to be photographed. While there may be many photo opportunities, there are a few things you can do to make sure you capture the best shots possible. For example, our shot in **Figure A** offers saturated colors, interesting reflections, and good composition to create a strong image.

A

The saturated colors and reflections in this shot make it a great way to show off the vibrant hues of autumn.

Pick the right time of day

What could be better than a sunny, vibrant blue sky on a cool October day? Well, even though this may sound idyllic, the best conditions for photographing fall colors might surprise you. The best time to shoot isn't when there's the most light. In fact, the early morning or late afternoon on a cloudy but bright day makes for great shots. When the sun is out, the colors are more likely to be washed out from overexposure. The cloud cover allows your digital camera to make more accurate exposure readings because the filtered, diffused light is cast evenly across the entire scene. This gives you better color accuracy and colors that are bright and clear.

One of the best times to capture lively autumn colors is immediately after a rain shower. Not only are you likely to have an overcast sky, but the rain will have cleaned the air and the leaves, giving you a clear shot of your scene. You can even take shots during the rain, as shown in **Figure B**, as long as you take care to protect your digital camera from the elements.

Framing your fall colors

When shooting the glories of fall, make sure your shots tell a story. Sweeping vistas of Technicolor® trees are nice, but we've all seen it before. Consider what you want to convey with your picture—what in the scene appeals to you? Concentrate on the details and then make your central subject easily identifiable, such as in **Figure C** on the next page.

B

Shooting during or after an autumn rainstorm can produce some great images.

Get up close

Don't be afraid to zoom in and get close to the essential elements in the scene. Instead of shooting an entire grove of colorful trees, isolate one tree or even go so far as to focus on one leaf. While the myriad colors sweeping across a panoramic landscape can be breathtaking, filling the frame with a central subject results in a more interesting photograph.

Look for patterns

Finally, autumn is a great time to search out interesting natural patterns and contrasts. With all the color and texture in the foliage, you'll find subtle variations in hue and intensity that adds visual drama to your shots, as shown in **Figure D**. Try juxtaposing the warm colors of the leaves with the neutral and cool tones of other natural objects, such as rocks and earth. Look for contrasts between different types of leaves as well as shadow and light areas. Remember to keep your composition simple—too much contrast can result in a discordant image. Use patterns to simplify a chaotic scene and, in turn, create a stronger image.

Setting up your camera

Just as important as selecting a good subject is making the correct settings on your camera to get the best exposure. Obviously, most of your autumn photography will take place outdoors, so forget about your flash. Instead, concentrate on your digital camera's exposure settings and rely on the natural lighting to get the best shot.

First, color easily washes out when overexposed, so it's best to lean toward underexposure when shooting. You can always boost the midtones and highlights in your image-editing program, but there isn't much you can do to fix an overexposed image.

One of the reasons morning is the best time to shoot fall colors is the low angle of the sun. When light is beating down on your subject, you'll have a tough time balancing out the highlights and the shadows. A low angle allows for more even lighting and offers less risk of overexposure.

A tripod is a must for many fall shots. Since you'll be using natural light and not a flash to illuminate your scene, there's

C

Make sure your subject is identifiable when shooting, such as this tree and its vivid reflection.

D

Autumn is a great time to photograph patterns in nature.

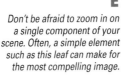

Don't be afraid to zoom in on a single component of your scene. Often, a simple element such as this leaf can make for the most compelling image.

E

a good chance you'll have to use a slower shutter speed to get enough light. Of course, the longer your shutter is open, the more likely you'll notice camera movement. However, using a tripod doesn't have to be limiting. Use it to get interesting angles and perspectives on your subject. The steady platform allows you to experiment with longer exposures and even panning techniques to create cool blur effects.

When zooming in on your subject, use your optical zoom to your advantage, but avoid using the digital zoom. Digitally zooming with your camera is the same as magnifying the image in an image-editing application and results in lower-quality images. If your camera has a macro mode, use it to get up close and personal with your subject, as we have in **Figure E**.

Finally, consider using some of the preprogrammed exposure settings on your camera. Often, you'll find a Scene or Landscape setting that adjusts your camera to take outdoor shots or a white balance setting specifically for cloudy or sunny days. If you have the ability to select your ISO sensitivity, use a lower setting, such as ISO 100 or 200, to reduce the possibility of digital noise developing. Lower ISOs also tend to create richer, more saturated colors.

Note: *When editing your images on your computer, consider boosting saturation levels to really make your colors pop.*

Overcoming the challenges of winter photography

Winter is a great time to get out and take some pictures with your digital camera. While there's certainly no shortage of subjects to capture, getting the shot right can be tricky. Variable light conditions, reflections off bright snow, and hazardous weather conditions combine to make winter the most challenging, yet rewarding, time of year to photograph.

Shoot for proper exposure

The light meter in your digital camera is a highly sophisticated piece of electronics, but it can be completely mystified by a bright field of snow. When shooting an intense scene like that, your camera tries to adjust for the midtone in the scene and will most likely underexpose slightly. The result is gray, murky-looking snow. This can be fixed by increasing the exposure compensation before you take the shot. How much of an increase depends on the lighting situation and the sensitivity of your camera, but a setting between +0.3 and +1.0 EV should do the trick. The slight overexposure returns the snow to its proper whiteness, as shown in **Figure A**.

Backlighting and silhouettes

The fine line between a portrait and a silhouette is another exposure challenge when dealing with backlighting. The brightness of a snowy background can cause details in your foreground to be washed out, creating a silhouette effect. If you're shooting for detail in your subject, position yourself so the background has less influence on your shot. Move in closer and fill the frame with your subject. If possible, reposition yourself to frame the subject against a background of trees or a building.

The importance of the time of day

The time of day can have a dramatic effect on your images, especially when you're shooting in snow. The early morning and later afternoon hours provide warm, pastel tones, while the bright light of midday offers cooler and more neutral tones, as shown in **Figure B**. If you're looking for color in your photography, avoid the middle

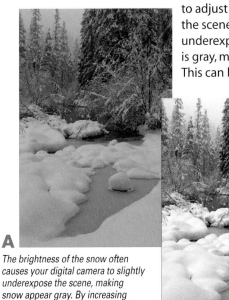

A

The brightness of the snow often causes your digital camera to slightly underexpose the scene, making snow appear gray. By increasing your exposure compensation, the whiteness of the snow can be accurately captured.

of the day and use the warm light of dawn and dusk to your advantage.

Throw some light on the subject

Conventional photographic wisdom states that your flash is pretty much useless outdoors. However, when shooting in snow, firing a flash can provide highlights and bring out details your camera might not have picked up on. The high reflection factor of the snow allows the flash to add texture and interest to a flat field of snow. The flash might also pick up any falling snow in the scene, adding depth and a sparkling sense of place, as shown in **Figure C**.

Many digital cameras have what is called *fill flash*. This type of flash works well in winter scenes, as it's designed to "fill" shadows and backlit subjects. You might also try using the Slow Synchronized (often called Slow Sync) option, if available. This flash mode is designed for poor lighting situations and works well if you're shooting later in the day. However, Slow Sync mode means that the camera's shutter automatically operates at slower speeds to capture the illumination behind the flash-lit subject, so using a tripod to reduce camera movement is recommended.

Note: *Avoid using flash when shooting close-up or macro shots with a bright background. The reflection greatly reduces any detail in your image and can cause distracting hotspots.*

B

The time of day can have a drastic effect on your winter shots. For cooler shots, shoot closer to midday, while shooting in the early morning and late afternoon results in warmer tones.

C

We captured the falling snow's sparkle by forcing the flash to fire.

Composing your shots

All the same rules apply when taking shots in winter, but there are a few techniques you can concentrate on to utilize the environmental conditions. While we've already discussed some of the technical aspects of winter photography, here's a list of some ways to compose your shots to do justice to the frosty scenes:

- **Look for contrasts.** Look for colorful subjects and textures to juxtapose against the monochromatic snow and gloomy winter skies.

- **Use the available light.** Light is scarce in the winter, so if you have the good fortune of dramatic lighting, seize the chance to get some interesting shots.

- **Shoot after a storm.** One of the best times to shoot in the winter is after a weather event. From a simple frost to a full-fledged blizzard, the aftermath can allow you to produce stunning photography. Subjects that were once mundane are now incredible, such as the ice-covered branches shown in **Figure D**, or high, sculpted snow drifts.

- **Use a filter.** Consider using a graduated filter to reduce the contrast between the sky and the ground, or use a polarizing filter to reduce reflections from the snow.

Don't get frozen when shooting in cold weather

Since digital cameras contain a number of delicate electrical and optical components, you should always take steps to protect yourself and your digital camera to ensure safe camera operation and good health for shooting when the temperatures get cold:

- **Understanding the challenges.** Extreme temperatures, whether hot or cold, can be hazardous to your camera's health, but by no means should you keep your digital camera indoors from November until April. By protecting the delicate elements and monitoring your camera's behavior when using it in cold weather, you can maintain reliable operation. Check your manual to find the optimal temperature range for your digital camera.

- **Take care of yourself first.** Keeping your body warm should be your primary concern, so make sure to have proper clothing on before heading out to shoot. Since you'll need your hands to operate your camera, consider using a pair of gloves that keep your hands warm without limiting your movement. Some photographers opt for fingerless gloves, which work well for digital cameras that have smaller buttons and controls that require finer dexterity. You'll also be dealing with slippery conditions, so providing yourself with a firm grip on the ground allows you to keep steady and avoid taking a tumble that can harm both you and your digital camera.

- **Avoid the battery deep freeze.** While you may think the digital camera itself is the most susceptible to cold, your batteries are actually the weakest part of the equation. Avoid alkaline batteries

D

Harsh weather like an ice storm can offer unique shooting opportunities.

when shooting in colder weather. They don't carry a high capacity charge and are drastically affected by cold temperatures. Instead, use NiMH (Nickel Metal Hydride) or Lithium Ion rechargeable batteries, which hold a stronger charge for a longer time and don't have as many problems in the cold.

- **Get yourself an external battery pack.** Not only does it provide ample power for a longer period of time, but it can also be kept in a coat pocket to keep it warm. This eliminates the problems associated with cold temperatures, but requires that your camera be tethered to a wire coming out of your pocket.

- **Keep the camera warm and dry.** Besides poor battery performance, your digital camera's greatest enemy is condensation. When you return to the warmth of your car or a building, the warm, humid air can produce condensation on your digital camera. It isn't the end of the world if you get a drop or two of moisture on your camera's body. However, if heavy condensation forms in the viewfinder, lens, or electronic components, you could turn your camera into an expensive paperweight or, at the very least, seriously compromise its functionality. Try to avoid the development of condensation by transitioning your digital camera from a cold to warm environment slowly. Keep the camera in a camera bag or coat pocket until it has a chance to come to room temperature.

- **Prevent condensation from happening.** Some digital photographers seal their digital cameras in plastic bags before transitioning from cold temperatures to warm. If condensation develops on your digital camera, remove as much excess moisture from the camera body as possible, but stay away from the camera's LCD panel, viewfinder, and lens. You're much better off waiting for this moisture to evaporate. And don't return the camera to the cold temperature to reverse the condensation effect. Not only doesn't this work, but it also could make the moisture freeze, causing massive mechanical and electrical problems.

- **Protect the camera from the elements.** There are weatherproof and waterproof shells designed to fit some of the more popular digital cameras. If you choose this option, make sure the shell gives you access to your controls and doesn't obscure the lens or viewfinder. Providing a dry place to store your camera is your first priority. While slipping the camera under your coat is always a good option, using a plastic bag to cover your camera is an inexpensive and more versatile way to protect the camera from precipitation. Cut holes in the bag for your viewfinder and lens and use rubber bands or tape to hold them in place.

Fast-action modes

Capturing fast action has always been a problem for digital cameras. Early digital models suffered from intolerably slow shutter lag, write times, and refresh rates. Those digital cameras seemed better suited for group shots and portraits than shooting any type of action. Today's digital cameras have overcome most of these problems and have added new features that make capturing the moment easier. One of these features is burst mode, where your camera takes several shots rapidly to record a series of images, as shown in **Figure A**. By using burst mode effectively, you can not only capture sequential shots, but you can also take several pictures of a scene and increase your chances of getting the perfect shot.

Bursting with pictures

We're using the term *burst mode*, but this feature is also called *continuous*, *sequential*, *multi-shot*, and a few other names. It can easily be compared to a motorwind on a film camera, where the film is quickly advanced to capture a series of images. At four or five frames per second (fps), you could blow through a roll of film very quickly, which wasn't always the intention of the more casual photographer. With digital technology, taking more pictures isn't only possible, but welcome. Instead of having to develop rolls of film to see your shots, you can burst your way through large numbers of shots without incurring additional cost.

Digital cameras still have a way to go before they match the burst capacity of a film camera, but the gap is narrowing. A film camera just needs a fast shutter and a quick motorwind, but a digital camera requires a few more complex components to get the shots. Let's examine which features are needed to make a digital camera burst, starting at the beginning of the process.

Short shutter lag

When you press the shutter button to take a picture, there's a brief but noticeable lag before the image is captured. *Shutter*

A

You can capture fast-moving action using the burst mode on your digital camera.

lag has decreased recently with faster autofocus systems and shorter exposure measurements, but it's still a factor. When shooting in burst mode, it's important to have a camera that has a short shutter lag or to set your camera to reduce this delay.

B

Digital camera manufacturers use buffers in different ways, but this diagram shows the basic process.

Fast recycle time

Recycle time is how long it takes your camera to be ready to take the next shot or burst of shots. In a burst mode, a digital camera usually sets focus and exposure on the first shot, and then takes the remaining shots in the sequence using those settings. This speeds up the recycle time, as time isn't spent re-evaluating the scene.

Your digital camera's recycle time also depends on how fast the image can be processed and written to your storage media. The faster your camera can write to your memory card, the more quickly you can capture your next shot. For this reason, many burst modes shoot images at less than the camera's maximum resolution to reduce the amount of information to process.

Large buffer memory

The burst rate of a digital camera largely depends on the size of its *buffer memory*. This memory stores image data before it's processed and saved to your storage media, as shown in **Figure B**. Since your camera doesn't have to wait between shots to save every image, you can take more images in a row. Professional digital cameras usually have very large buffers, as applications such as sports

photography require a large amount of space for many sequential images.

Many frames per second

All of these factors determine how many frames per second your digital camera is capable of shooting. Camera manufacturers seem to have two types of systems in place when shooting in burst mode. In one type, the number of shots you can take in a burst sequence is limited. For example, the Canon G5 takes 2.5 frames per second for a maximum of eight frames, which is likely the maximum capacity of that camera's buffer. The other type of burst mode allows you to shoot until the buffer is full, and then continue to shoot as soon as the buffer space is freed up. As long as the shutter button is pressed, this type of burst mode continues to take images until the batteries run out or the storage media is filled.

Know your timing

Most digital cameras allow you to preset shutter and exposure settings by pressing the shutter button halfway down and holding it. When in burst mode, this can help reduce the shutter

lag time and give you a better chance to get the right shot.

Focus on infinity

As we mentioned earlier, many burst modes set the focus for the first shot and maintain that focus through the remaining shots. This can be problematic with moving objects, which have a tendency to move out of the focal plane. This can even be a problem when you preset the focus using the half-pressed button technique. One solution is to set your camera to focus on infinity, which usually sets up your camera to have a large focal plane. This works best for situations, such as shooting from the sidelines of a sporting event, where there's some distance between the camera and the subject.

Know your place

Capturing the moment is as much a matter of being in the right place at the right time as it is setting your camera appropriately. Anticipate where the action is going to take place and be ready to shoot when your subject reaches your target spot. If possible, try to be parallel to the action so the movement is from side to side and not coming directly toward you or

C

Burst shots are best taken when the action is moving parallel to the camera, but you can get good shots of subjects moving away from you if you plan your shot correctly.

going away from you. However, if you plan your shot carefully, you can create some interesting series, such as the sledding shots in **Figure C**.

Pan for gold

When shooting fast-moving objects in burst mode, you

D

Panning is the key to getting smooth motion when shooting action shots.

should try to track your subject smoothly by pointing your camera at the action and following it as closely as possible. This technique is known as *panning*, and not only does it help to keep your subject in focus, but it also offers a better sense of movement in the image. **Figure D** shows a shot panned from a single fixed location, but moving along with the action can also yield good results if you can keep a steady hand. You can use tripods while panning, especially when you have a good idea of where the action will take place. When in doubt, try handholding your camera, which gives you more flexibility to quickly adjust the framing of your shot.

Select a lower resolution

This is a recommendation that's rare, but if capturing a large number of images is important, reducing the resolution of the images captured reduces image processing and saves time. This may not be an option with your digital camera, as many have a preset resolution for images taken in burst mode. Again, consult your manual and find out how your camera handles the resolution of burst images.

Taking silhouettes

A silhouette is a classic and dramatic photographic technique. By isolating the outline of a subject while eliminating detail, a silhouette places tremendous emphasis on shape and contrast. It isn't only popular for portrait photography, but also landscapes and nature photography. While traditional SLRs create a silhouetted shot with a manual exposure adjustment, the automatic nature of digital cameras makes achieving this effect more difficult. However, it isn't impossible to shoot silhouettes with your digital camera if you follow a few simple guidelines.

An extreme contrast

A *silhouette* is defined as an outline of something that appears dark against a lighter background. This usually occurs by exposing for the background, which underexposes the subject and produces a silhouette. Some silhouettes completely erase discernible detail in the subject, while some allow small areas of detail around the edges of the subject to maintain depth. As we mentioned earlier, the use of silhouettes is a great portrait technique when isolating identifying characteristics, such as a nose or a chin, but silhouettes can be equally powerful when shooting more natural shots, as the example shown in **Figure A**. A tree branch backlit by the moon, a surfer walking the beach at dawn, or a bird juxtaposed

A

Using silhouettes is a great technique to isolate form when you want to create dramatic results.

against the setting sun are all wonderful ways to use silhouettes to create a particular mood in your photography.

Setting up a silhouette

When preparing to photograph a silhouette, all you have to do is be aware of a few simple rules to make sure your composition is strong. Incorrect framing or exposure of a silhouette can zap it of all its straightforward power, so take the time to get the shot right.

A little background

While the subject of your shot is the most important element of your image, it doesn't have a chance of being noticed if you choose an inappropriate background. A good background for a silhouette should be simple, evenly well-lit, and of a fairly neutral color. Many of the most powerful silhouettes are displayed in black and white, but colored backgrounds can be effective if they aren't distracting. An uncluttered background highlights the outline's finer details while providing enough light to give emphasis to the outline, as shown in **Figure B**. Excellent natural backgrounds include snow, water, and all phases of the sky (sunset, sunrise, cloudy, etc.) because they're of a uniform texture and luminosity. If you choose to shoot against a background with a greater texture, such as a brick wall, choose subjects with a bold outline so the finer details don't get lost.

B

Good backgrounds, such as the sky in this shot, don't detract from your silhouetted form.

C

By metering the sky in the area indicated by the crosshairs, we were able to underexpose the subject and create the silhouette.

Positioning your subject

Once you've decided on a background, the next step is to position your subject to emphasize an identifying feature. The most important consideration is to place your subject so it's appropriately backlit and so that it stands out from the background. Keep the shape simple and try to avoid having it run out of the frame. Eliminate as much foreground lighting as possible, such as artificial lights or reflections from natural light, as it might add detail to your silhouetted subject. If you're shooting a subject that blocks the light source, make sure that the light is appropriately hidden or your silhouette edges could have distracting hotspots. Unless, of course, that's what you want!

Capturing the silhouette

Capturing a silhouette is really a matter of setting the camera's exposure for the bright background, so we'll need to trick the camera into adjusting to underexpose the foreground. Since digital cameras rarely have the same features, we'll show you a few different approaches for setting your digital camera to get the silhouette effect.

Put the flash in the pan

Since your background is providing the light for your image, you won't need to use your camera's on-board flash. If your flash is left on, the camera will most likely fire it off when you take your shot to correctly expose the scene. Some portrait photographers like to use a flash to subtly light the sides of a subject, but in most cases it's better to just turn your flash off.

The magic of the half-pressed button

Most digital cameras employ a two-stage attack when you press the shutter button. The first, when the button is half pressed, allows the camera to meter the scene, set focus, perform white balance, and a whole host of other processes that automatically set the exposure for the shot. When the button is then fully pressed, the camera opens the shutter and captures the shot according to these settings. To trick the camera into underexposing the foreground, you'll need to use the half-pressed button technique to your advantage.

To use the half-pressed button technique:

1. Point your camera at the background.

2. Press the shutter button halfway down to get the correct exposure.

3. Reframe your shot while still holding the button halfway down.

4. Fully depress the shutter button to take the shot once your subject is framed. The camera properly exposes the background while underexposing the foreground, producing a silhouette of your subject.

Figure C shows the scene from **Figure B** metered directly in the center of the subject, as well as the location we chose to meter to achieve the silhouette effect.

Focus concerns

While half-pressing the button sets the exposure you want, it also sets the focus. Since few digital cameras have manual focus, it's understandable that this might be a concern. One thing to remember is that you want your background to have clarity, but it's less important that the foreground object is in focus. The only responsibility of the subject is to provide a good amount of contrast from the background to isolate its shape. If you want more control over the focal range of your camera, play around with your camera's focus modes, such as counterweighted or spot metered. Not all cameras have them, so check your camera's manual if you're unsure.

Exposure lock

Some cameras give you the ability to customize your exposure by locking in exposure readings. This allows you to override the automatic setting and shoot exclusively with your own desired exposure. This feature is usually buried in your camera's menu, so again check out your manual if you're unsure whether your digital camera has this feature. While it won't make or break your silhouette, the exposure lock feature can make it easier to get the right shot.

Exposure compensation

Almost every digital camera has some form of exposure compensation. This feature

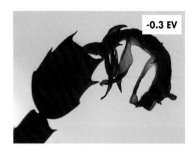

-0.3 EV

-0.7 EV

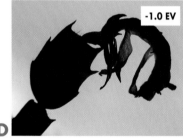

-1.0 EV

D

You can create better silhouettes by decreasing the exposure level on your camera.

allows the user to increase or decrease the camera's sensitivity to light. This can come in handy with silhouettes, especially if your camera is still giving you detail in your subject even after you've set the exposure for the bright background. By setting the exposure compensation in negative numbers, your camera underexposes the shot overall and minimizes the details in your subject, as illustrated in **Figure D**.

Other options

There are quite a few more options to tweak on your camera to get a silhouette just right, but they depend on the capacity of your camera. Some cameras offer a specific picture mode that adjusts your camera to take a silhouette. Others offer manual control over your exposure system that can help get the right shot. When setting these manual controls, keep in mind that a good silhouette comes from a fast shutter speed, a slower

aperture, negative exposure compensation, and a higher film speed. Take advantage of every feature your camera has and find out which setting works best for you.

Silhouette shooting style

Take as many shots as you have memory, to give you the widest range of shots to choose from. Experiment with different exposure settings—you can always check the EXIF data later to see what the settings were when you captured that perfect silhouette. Try changing your point of view or rearranging your subject to emphasize the most identifiable features. Remember that your LCD preview screen is your best friend in situations like these—no more waiting until your film gets processed to see your results. This digital camera standard feature is the best way to make sure you get the correct shot while you're still at the scene. And, as always, it's a good idea to use a tripod to minimize camera vibrations and ensure that your subject's edges are distinct.

Macrophotography

If you've heard the term *macrophotography* and have thought it's some sort of digital photo software, well, you should think again. The term *macro* means large, so you might conclude the term means large photographs. No, that isn't quite it, because the term actually refers to how the subjects appear in the photographs—large, close-up, and very personal.

Although the principles behind macrophotography are in every sense the same as ordinary photography, there's nothing ordinary about the results. That's because macrophotography takes the ordinary and captures it from an extraordinary viewpoint, as shown in **Figure A**. If you've long wanted to try macrophotography, there's no better time than now. Macro features are standard on many digital cameras today, so if you've never been any closer to a subject than three feet away, move in and explore the exciting world of macrophotography.

It's a macro, macro world

Macrophotography is similar to normal photography, with one main exception. You're working very close to your subject. Generally, this means the reproduction size of your image (i.e., the size of your image when focused on your CCD) falls in a range of 1:2 to 1:1. Anything

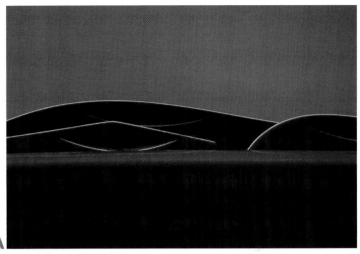

A

Macrophotography can provide an extraordinary viewpoint to ordinary subjects.

closer than 1:1 is considered microphotography.

Technically, macrophotography is the same as normal photography. You must control lighting, exposure, framing, focus, and subject material if you wish to produce a successful photo. However, there's one difference that you must keep in mind if you wish to create a worthwhile image—scale.

Because you're so close to your subject, details have greater importance, and your actions have greater consequences. You adjust your framing an eighth of an inch and it looks like eight inches in your viewfinder. You move closer to your subject by a quarter-inch and your entire composition goes out of focus. Next, we'll provide a few tips to help you master the macro world.

Master the macro maladies

Perhaps the greatest problem you'll encounter as you experiment with macro-photography is movement—movement of not only your subject, but of your camera as well. You can make the slightest camera adjustment, and your subject disappears from your viewfinder. Given this vital consideration, your priority is to stabilize your camera, which means a tripod is essential. Even if your subject is completely still, such as our example in **Figure B**, the slightest camera movement will not only degrade your image quality but the composition as well.

Keep it steady

It's also paramount that you stabilize your subject. Obviously, subjects you photograph indoors, such as coins, marbles, or buttons, present few

B

Macrophotography requires a tripod, for even slight camera movements can degrade image quality.

C

Lighting macro subjects requires as much skill as lighting large subjects, only the tools are smaller.

problems with motion. However, macrophotography may frequently take you outdoors, and even inanimate objects, such as flowers or plants, can be extremely difficult to keep in focus when there's even the slightest breeze. So, in addition to a tripod, you should always plan to take a few items with you to secure your subject(s), such as dowels, pencils, string, twist ties, and even tape. Animate subjects, chiefly insects, are an entirely different topic.

Provide ample light

You also have to properly light your subject. Approach lighting as you would when taking a portrait. Portrait lighting is used to bring out the best features in large subjects (e.g., adults, kids, and pets). Think about bringing out the best features in your small subjects, such as nickels, walnuts, and even peppercorns. The same lighting principles apply as with portrait photography, which means you may use main, fill, rim lights, and reflector flats. However, instead of using professional lighting, you use mini flashlights, pocket mirrors, and note cards, to get the results shown in **Figure C**.

You also have to be patient. When working at the macro level, don't be a bull in a china shop. Think about making slight adjustments and move carefully. Settle down, take your time, and mentally focus on your macro world.

Working around autofocus

The intention of the autofocus feature of a digital camera is to free you from the responsibility of setting focus and improving the quality of your images. However honorable this intention may be, there are some situations when autofocus may not be your best ally, such as an off-center subject or a scene with low light. With a majority of digital cameras having only an autofocus optical system, learning how to beat the system will allow you to get these shots and open new creative techniques to explore.

How autofocus works

Let's examine how the autofocus system works. Digital cameras employ a number of focusing technologies to produce a clear picture. Some use an *active* autofocus system that emits an infrared light to measure the distance between the camera and the subject. The processor on the camera uses the distance measurement to adjust the focus motor behind the lens to bring that distance into focus. Others use a *passive* autofocus system, wherein the image sensor "looks" at the scene and sets focus based on various distances and color contrasts. Others measure subjects in certain areas of the frame and make adjustments according to preset focus values, such as multi AF (autofocus), center AF, or spot AF.

Regardless of the focusing system on your digital camera, there are situations where you're going to have to trick it. If a scene is too dark, the infrared beam may be absorbed. If the subject is moving too fast, the image sensor might not have enough time to make an appropriate adjustment. We aren't going to concentrate on any particular autofocus system, as they all can be "fooled" in essentially the same way.

Good shots are a lock

Most autofocus digital cameras allow you to focus the camera automatically to a comparable subject, lock that focal range, and reframe the shot using the desired subject. You can do this by pressing the shutter button halfway to lock the focus, which locks the exposure settings as well. Then, you can point the camera in any direction and it will maintain the focus and exposure values. This is the essence of the trick—by using the camera's autofocus mechanism to your advantage, you can still get those difficult shots.

Capturing off-center subjects

A common use for focus lock is capturing an off-center subject. In **Figure A**, our intended subject, the plant, is ignored for the much more prevalent brick background. Since the

Straight shot

Focus locked on hand

Final shot

A

By locking focus on another object, we were able to present our off-center subject with clarity, while the background is blurred.

Lack of contrast

Illuminated to lock focus

Final shot

B

For this shot, the light from a flashlight provided the illumination needed to lock the digital camera's focus mechanism.

subject is fairly small and we wanted to maintain the same framing, we couldn't easily place the plant in the center frame, lock focus, and then reframe the shot. Instead, we put a hand on the same vertical plane as the plant and locked the focus. Then, we took our hand away and captured the image. Even though our hand isn't there, the plant remains in focus and the background becomes less dominant. While the steady execution of this shot was aided by the use of a tripod, you could easily use this technique while handholding your camera.

Shooting in low light

One of the big problems of focusing in a scene of low light is the lack of contrast. Without contrasts, the autofocus system on the camera gets confused about what to focus on in your intended shot. As a result, your digital camera will usually prevent you from taking any shots at all. Nighttime photographers get around this by using the manual focus (if available) or setting the camera focus range to infinity. If you don't have manual focus or want to take a close-up shot, consider carrying around a flashlight or headlamp to illuminate your object. Even the low light of a flashlight provides enough contrast for the camera to work with, as shown in **Figure B**. Remember that using the flashlight is going to tweak your exposure readings, so it's best to use this technique when setting the exposure manually.

Note: *Autofocus systems can also be confused in scenes where there is a lack of contrast, which can be caused by bright light, strong reflections, or foggy conditions. In these situations, lock focus on a darker area of the scene (in the same distance plane) that contains more contrast.*

Working with mixed subjects

Another situation that can cause autofocus systems to get confused is when the subjects are mixed. For example, consider a shot that involves two off-center subjects on a busy background. The camera doesn't know whether to focus on the background, foreground, or just split the difference and measure the center of the image. You can remedy this situation by using the focus-lock technique. Instead of asking the camera to average all of the elements in the shot, recompose the picture so the focal plane is in the center, lock focus, reframe the shot to the original composition, and take the shot.

Taking action shots

Focus lock can come in handy when you're trying to capture subjects that are moving. Often, there isn't enough time for the camera to process the scene and correctly focus on a moving object. Instead, the key is to anticipate your shot and be prepared. By locking focus on another subject in the same distance range as your intended shot, you can be ready for the action and catch a moment like the one shown in **Figure C**.

The effects of depth of field

When using focus lock, be aware that it also has a lot to do with depth of field. Simply put, while you're setting your critical focus on a certain object, there will be areas in front of and behind the object that will appear in focus. Your goal when using focus lock is to ensure that your subject or subjects are sharp. Sometimes, you'll have to take a gamble and hope for the best. Make sure you shoot a lot of pictures and use your LCD screen to preview your images. Then, you'll be better in tune with the nuances of your camera.

Note: *If you want to increase your depth of field, use a smaller aperture (larger f-stop number). To have a shallow depth of field, use a larger aperture (smaller f-stop number).*

C

We captured this shot by locking the focus on the woman and anticipating the moment the tennis ball reached the same focal plane.

Manual focusing

In the past 15 years, autofocus technology has become very good. So good in fact that you could assume digital camera manufacturers figure that most users aren't going to want to mess around with focus rings when the programmed precision of autofocus does the job. Manual focus capabilities are currently reserved for only the most expensive digital cameras, and manufacturers have turned their attention to other user demands, such as improved image quality and larger megapixel sizes.

But as digital photography matures, people are expecting more from their digital cameras. Let's take a look at some of the situations that lend themselves to focusing manually.

Shooting in low light
Low light is like Kryptonite to autofocus. When lighting conditions are insufficient, autofocus mechanisms and programming can't collect enough information to evaluate the scene and set focus. Most likely, your digital camera will continually re-evaluate the scene, never deciding on a set focal range. Manual focus gives the photographer control over the focal plane when low-light levels render autofocus useless, as is the case in **Figure A**.

Shooting a fast-moving subject
Shutter lag is a big issue with digital cameras, as it causes the shutter to fire a split second after you push the shutter button. In that split second, the camera is evaluating exposure, setting white balance, and focusing the lens, but by then your photographic moment might have disappeared. By setting your focus manually for where you expect the action to take place, you can eliminate some of the lag and put yourself in a better position to get the shot, as was done in **Figure B**.

Shooting macro shots
When you get up close and personal with your subject, focusing can become a problem for an automatic system. A digital camera set for macro mode has a narrow range of focus, so autofocus only has a limited space in your scene that it can use. By manually focusing your macro shots, you have a much better chance of getting the shot in focus and controlling

A

By switching over to manual focus, we were able to get this low-light shot.

the depth of field to capture the right plane in your scene. We cover this concept in more detail later on.

Shooting for artistic effect

Manual focus is an essential part of professional photography because it allows the photographer to have complete control over each shot. Slight shifts in focus can cause major shifts in the central subject of an image. Using manual focus allows the photographer to better lead the viewer's eye through the image.

Manual focus options for digital cameras

There are three main categories of manual focus for digital cameras. As you can expect, the shift from film to digital caused many camera manufacturers to rethink manual focus, so learning how to use the new setups can be a challenge, but one that can be easily overcome with practice.

Full manual control

This is the common manual control you'd expect on a traditional SLR. A focus ring is located on the lens that allows you to adjust the lens. This type of focusing system is found on higher-end digital cameras, whose prices are typically in the $1,000+ range. However, as digital SLRs become more prevalent in the next few years, look for these systems to become much more common at the sub-$1,000 level.

B

Autofocus often isn't fast enough to capture fast-moving action, where manual focus gives you a better chance.

Stepped manual control

Most digital cameras that claim manual focus abilities actually use a system unique to digital cameras. Instead of using a focus ring to adjust the lens, the user selects preset focal ranges from menus on the camera. For example, the Nikon 4500 has a manual focus mode that allows the user to select from 50 preset focal settings, ranging from 1.3 feet to infinity. Setting focus is a matter of choosing the correct range, positioning the camera, and using the LCD or optical viewfinder to check for sharpness. This manual focus option isn't as flexible as full manual, but it does offer control over an otherwise fixed lens and helps the manufacturer keep the price of the camera down.

Faking manual focus

Okay, this isn't really a true category of manual focus, but it's important to consider nonetheless. Even if your digital camera has a fully automatic manual focus system, you can still have some control over what your camera is focusing on. When you half-press the shutter button, your digital camera sets the focus for the shot and maintains it until the shutter is fully pressed or released. Once the focus is set, you can reposition the camera to focus on a different subject, provided that you keep the shutter button half-pressed. This is a great technique for macro shots where your autofocus can't quite get it right, as shown in **Figure C**. By locking the focus and moving the camera slightly, you can refocus the shot and capture the details you're after.

Shooting with manual focus

There are a few challenges you'll face when manually focusing your digital camera, but nothing

C

Even with a fully automatic digital camera, you can manually influence the focal plane and get difficult shots like this extreme macro.

you can't overcome with a little practice. By setting your digital camera's controls correctly and carefully framing your shots, you can get the hang of manual focus and use it to your advantage.

Trusting your eyes

Most digital cameras have an LCD panel used for previewing the image, but many have an optical viewfinder that can also be used. When using autofocus, you trust the accuracy of how the camera is focusing, but you'll have to rely on your own eyes when using manual focus. This means you'll have to use your viewing options to decide whether the shot is in focus. While LCD panels are small and low-resolution, you can get a good idea of whether your image is in focus. When in doubt, take the shot, preview the image on the LCD screen, and use the preview zoom feature to check focus. You'll never really know until you view the image on your monitor, but at the very least you'll be able to fix big problems while still in front of your scene.

Note: Some digital cameras have diopter adjustments to adjust the optical viewfinder to the user's eyesight. Make sure you make this adjustment before you switch to manual focusing or it will be much harder to set precise focus.

Controlling depth of field

The smaller the aperture number is (for example, f/2.4), the smaller the depth of field in your shot. Depth of field is the area in your shot that is in focus, and it conversely increases as you use larger apertures, such as f/8. Knowing how aperture selection affects the depth of field in your shot is very important for understanding what focal range you can expect. For this reason, we recommend using Aperture Priority mode when shooting with manual focus. This allows you to make the decisions about aperture and focal range, while the camera sets the shutter speed to its optimal setting.

D

The Focus Confirmation feature highlights the edges of your image in the LCD preview to show you what's in focus. Note the white highlights on the veins of the leaf.

Prefocusing the shot

If you plan to use manual focusing to capture fast-moving action, you should prefocus your shot. This can be as simple as estimating the physical distance between you and the expected location of your subject, or you can place an object in that spot, set focus, and wait for the action to occur. For digital cameras with stepped manual focusing, prefocusing is a must for capturing fast action, but even those lucky enough to have a focus ring can benefit from planning their focus ahead. Even if the shot isn't perfectly sharp, it will only take a small adjustment of the ring to bring your subject into focus.

Using Focus Confirmation

Some digital cameras have a feature known as Focus Confirmation, which provides visual confirmation of which areas of your shot are in focus by making the edges of focused areas look sharp. As shown in **Figure D**, the LCD screen shows an image that looks like it has lower resolution and higher contrast than normal, but this preview isn't transferred to your captured image. This feature could be very useful when in manual focus mode, so check your camera's manual for availability and test it out yourself.

Keeping the camera steady

Be aware of your camera settings and use a tripod if camera shake in your shot is a possibility. Shutter speeds under 1/60 of a second are typically considered ripe for camera shake, while higher shutter speeds are fast enough to overcome it. Since the concept of using manual focus is to bring your subject into the sharpest focus possible, don't risk degrading the image by not properly steadying the camera.

Controlling exposure priority

Most digital cameras have some level of manual control over exposure (some more than others). The control is usually over which mechanism of the exposure process gets priority—the shutter or the lens aperture. In either case, a balance between the two must exist to get a proper exposure—at least, the exposure you're trying to achieve. While these controls work together, they can produce different images. Are you trying to create a wide depth of field? Do you want to freeze sharp, focused images of high-speed action? Understanding how to use your digital camera's priority modes is the key to getting professional results in a variety of shooting situations.

Back to basics

To understand aperture and shutter priority, it's best to start with some of the fundamentals of photography.

Without an understanding of how these crucial processes function, it would be next to impossible to make intelligent choices on how to set them. In addition, comparing digital and traditional photography isn't always apples to apples, so being sensitive to the differences is crucial to getting consistent images.

Aperture

Aperture is the opening that allows light to pass through the lens. Apertures are usually expressed in f-stops—smaller f-stops represent larger apertures. A larger lens opening lets more light hit the CCD of the digital camera, to the tune of twice as much light for each full f-stop increase. This is why aperture control is so important for photographers who work in low-light and natural light situations. Without it, they'd have to use artificial light to create a proper exposure, which might spoil the mood of the shot.

A

In this shot, the depth of field is set for a narrow range to focus on only a portion of the scene.

B

By setting a slower shutter speed, we created the illusion of moving water in this river shot.

Depth of field

Aperture also controls the depth of field for your image. *Depth of field* is the distance between the closest and farthest objects in focus. A larger aperture, such as f/2, produces a shallower depth of field than a smaller aperture, such as f/11. This range of sharpness is also affected by the "film speed" and focal length of your lens, but the most important aspect of the depth of field of your scene is your aperture setting.

Why is depth of field important? Think about a portrait shot—you want the subject to be in sharp focus while the background blurs away. In that case, you'd want to use a large aperture. A smaller aperture would make more of the elements in the scene come into focus, making your subject less special.

Figure A illustrates how depth of field affects a shot. In the image, the depth of field is set so the middle two oranges are in focus, while the others blur away. By using depth of field to control the focal range, you can create a tension between objects in your scene and create more interesting images.

Using aperture priority

Aperture priority lets you set the aperture manually while the camera adjusts the shutter speed automatically. The main reason to use aperture priority is to control the depth of field without compromising the exposure. Designating a specific aperture can also help maintain the main focal point of your scene, as you can control the varying levels of sharpness. It also can be used to override the automatic settings when a poorly lit scene requires a larger opening to let in a greater amount of light.

The main reason to avoid using aperture priority is that objects in motion may come out blurry. Since the camera has to make the decision on how to balance the aperture with the shutter speed, often the shutter has to stay open longer to collect the correct amount of light, leading to a blurry image.

Most digital cameras have been shrunk to the smallest size possible. One of the costs of this compact size is a short lens with a short focal length. This allows the maximum amount of focus in a scene, but makes controlling specific focal ranges difficult. Using the aperture priority mode to set the lens opening for the shot can give you a level of control over the depth of field in your shots.

Using shutter priority

Most digital camera users understand that the *shutter speed* is how long the shutter is open, which controls the amount of time that light can hit the CCD of the digital camera. Shutter speeds are expressed in seconds—actually, they're usually expressed as fractions of a second. The slower the shutter speed, or greater the number of seconds, the more blurred and undefined the image becomes. The faster the shutter speed, the greater the ability to "freeze" the scene without the effects of blurring. Faster shutter speeds, usually those at 1/250 or less, can also eliminate any of the natural shakiness of your hands when you hold the camera, giving you sharper images.

Shutter priority allows you to set the shutter speed while the camera automatically controls the aperture. This gives you the ability to freeze fast-moving objects in your scene, but at the price of a reduced depth of field. Shutter priority is often used to capture the fast moving action of a sporting event (fast shutter speed) or to create the illusion of movement by blurring the moving portions of the image (slow shutter speed), as in a shot of a river shown in Figure B.

Note: *Some digital cameras have a full manual mode. This allows you to set everything, including the aperture and shutter speed, independently. These cameras are usually on the high end and require a better understanding of these topics.*

Which do you choose?

The exposure priority mode you choose depends entirely on the subject of your image. If you're taking shots at a sporting event and the automatic settings aren't cutting it, consider using shutter priority and accepting the narrower depth of field. If you need to control the depth of field in your image, aperture priority is for you. Neither one is better than the other, just better suited for different shooting situations.

Exposure bracketing

It's a once-in-a-lifetime shot—a colorful sunset fading away across the slow-moving waves of the ocean, perfectly silhouetting a lonely sailboat. You don't want to miss capturing this moment, but the tricky light levels are making the decision on the correct exposure settings a nerve-wracking endeavor. What do you do? You can rely on a technique known as *bracketing*, where you take several shots of the same scene at different exposures. While traditional photographers usually have to manually change the exposure settings to bracket their shots, most digital cameras have automated this process to make it very easy to use. With bracketing, you can reduce the chance that you'll miss that unique shot by increasing the range of exposures you capture.

In this three-shot bracket, the exposure values are -0.3, 0.0, and +0.3. You can have a broader range, but a narrow bracket gives you a better chance of getting it right.

> Note: *While you can bracket by adjusting shutter speed, aperture, or ISO settings, most digital cameras use positive or negative exposure compensation to vary the exposure.*

Shooting smart

When shooting a typical bracketed sequence, one shot is taken at the metered setting, one shot is underexposed, and one shot is overexposed, as shown in **Figure A**. One of the impediments of using exposure bracketing with traditional film cameras is that it "wastes" film. While you might think that getting the perfect shot outweighs the burning of a few frames of film, the fact remains that for every shot you select from a bracketed sequence, there will be three or more shots that are useless. However, digital cameras are limited only by the amount of storage—you can erase unnecessary images without any wasted resources.

When should you bracket?

Any shooting situation when you're second-guessing your metering ability is a good time to bring out the bracketing. These situations usually involve a scene that contains a wide range of lighting levels or a dramatic contrast between subject and background. Consider a scene where the background is a bright snow-covered field. For the subject to be properly exposed, your camera might decide to blow out the details in the background. Conversely, if you're shooting a particularly bright foreground subject, any negative exposure compensation applied to even out the exposure could reduce the amount of detail in your shadows.

For example, consider our ocean sunset image. The rapidly changing light of a sunset, as well as the reflections from the water, can make selecting an appropriate exposure difficult. By shooting at a variety of exposures, you have a better chance of capturing a correctly exposed shot.

Bracketing concerns

Before you bracket a series of shots, there are a few things to consider. First, since you'll be varying the exposure levels of the shots, it's a good idea to avoid your flash. You want to use the available light and make adjustments from there—using the flash will skew your results. Next, be aware of your mode setting. Exposure variations are different depending on whether you're using an aperture priority, a shutter priority, or a custom camera mode. Experiment first so you know what to expect from each mode. Finally, use a tripod to keep the camera steady and the scene consistent, as focus and white balance are typically measured on the first shot and not changed until the bracket sequence is complete.

Setting up an exposure bracket

Every digital camera, while technically performing the same procedure, seemingly has a different exposure bracketing procedure. The big differences from camera to camera are in the number of shots taken, the range of exposure values, and whether the bracketed shots are taken automatically or if they require you to manually push the shutter button. Consult your camera's manual to find out the capabilities of your camera.

For our example, we're going to use a digital camera that allows us to shoot three or five bracketed shots at +/- 0.3, +/- 0.6, or +/- 1.0 increments. We selected five shots at +/- 0.3, as it gives us a good range of shots without getting too dramatic from shot to shot. You aren't looking to have radically different bracketed shots, as the extreme exposures are almost sure to go too far.

This digital camera requires you to hold the shutter button down while it takes the series of shots. Once the five shots are taken, the shutter stops opening and you can release the shutter button. Some cameras automatically shoot all bracketed shots with one click of the shutter button, while others require you to click it for each shot. The bracketed sequence we captured is shown in **Figure B**.

Bracketing your shots manually

If your camera doesn't have automatic exposure bracketing but has adjustable exposure compensation, you can manually set up your own bracket. The technique here is to take one shot, allowing the camera to meter the scene. Then, take one shot at positive exposure compensation and one shot at negative exposure compensation. You get the same results—the automatic exposure bracketing just speeds the process along. While having your camera do all the work is easier, the benefit of manually bracketing your shot is that you aren't limited to the range of exposure you can shoot with.

Bracketed shots in post-process

Bracketing shots can also be helpful if you want to combine two images to get the best composite image. Let's go back to the subject in the snow—by taking a series of shots at different exposures, you can select a foreground subject that has the correct exposure from one shot with the background that contains good detail from another shot. Then, by combining these two elements, you can build a better composite shot. Often, this is the only way to make certain shots work, so keep it in mind when you shoot.

B *By shooting with a five-shot bracket, we were able to see the exposure extremes for this scene.*

Keeping your composition simple

One of the easiest and most efficient ways to improve your photography is to apply a few rules of photographic composition. The first, and easiest to understand, is the rule of simplicity. Too many elements in an image will draw the viewer's eyes all over a photograph, while centering in on one or two main elements will create a clear, direct visual message. By isolating the subject, through color or position of the camera, your image will become stronger and you'll be more pleased with your shots.

Producing simple images

How do you accomplish simplicity? It's largely a result of your shooting technique:

- When framing a shot, avoid cluttered backgrounds that might detract from your message.

- Choose a simple subject and include only enough of its surroundings to establish context.

- Try to avoid using several different colors. Instead, choose two or three colors that contrast well against each other.

- When aiming for simplicity, it never hurts to have a few dozen shots to pick from that represent different points of view. If you're shooting horizontally, take a few shots vertically.

- Try changing your point of view. By simply moving the camera over a bit and framing the subject tighter, you can change the whole feel of an image.

- Use the Gaussian Blur filter in Adobe Photoshop to blur a background and simplify an image to its main element.

- Simplify an image by designating an uncomplicated color scheme where minor changes in hue create pleasing contrasts.

- Employ your digital camera's Close Up mode, which gives a better focus range for tighter shots.

Achieving balance in your images

Sometimes a photograph can be a decent representation of the subject the photographer is trying to capture, but it distinctly lacks drama. One of the main causes of this problem is an unbalanced image. The concept of balance is a major aspect of good photographic composition and can help transform an average shot into an exceptional image. Understanding some simple concepts of balance will help improve the quality of the images you take with your digital camera.

Balance and image composition

In photography, *balance* is the relationship between your main subject and the other elements in the image, such as background, props, surroundings, and other subject matter. A majority of images employ one central subject—how that subject sits in the given space and interacts with other objects in the scene creates balance. The human mind seeks out balance, so an image with a sense of equilibrium draws and maintains our ever-shifting attention. By using balance, a good photographer delivers a clear message in a visually stimulating way.

Digital technology and balance

Digital cameras offer several features that encourage the creation of balanced shots. For example, the LCD screen allows the photographer to frame a shot precisely without having to wait for the film to process. Plus, the shot preview gives instant feedback on whether you accomplished your photographic goal. A digital camera provides you with more flexibility to experiment and find that perfectly balanced composition.

Types of balance

While there are many terms used to describe balance in image composition, there are two main categories to consider. Let's get to know the two types of balance.

Symmetrical balance

Many subjects offer a symmetrical composition. Balance is achieved through this symmetry, as shown in **Figure A**. This type of balance is often referred to as *formal balance*, as each side of the photograph has equal weight and similar colors and contrast. It's also called formal because it's a stiff composition technique.

A

A computer composition with symmetrical balance offers equilibrium from each side of the image.

Symmetrical balance should be used for images that lend themselves to a more structured composition, such as group shots or documentary photography.

Asymmetrical balance

While symmetrical balance certainly creates a complementary arrangement of subjects, some photographers believe it separates the image in two or more parts, and in effect, divides the viewer's attention. Asymmetrical balance, or *informal balance*, offsets different objects in a scene to create a more stimulating visual experience. The dynamic placement of elements offers balance by placing the center of interest away from the visual center of the picture. In **Figure B**, the main focus of the photograph is the off-center bowl in the foreground, yet the out-of-focus bowl in the background offers balance.

Counterbalance

Another aspect of asymmetrical balance is using a smaller counter object to balance your larger subject. In **Figure C**, we see an image of a mysteriously lit book. The image of the book in the middle of our frame would be boring on its own, even with the lights splayed over it. Balancing the large book with smaller elements helps with the composition. The careful addition of the stones and glasses takes some of the book's initial visual weight off the image and spreads it out over the entire frame.

Other balancing acts

Equally important to the balance of objects in your scene is the balance of colors and textures. Obviously, if you're shooting in black and white, your color options might not be as important, but even then the range of contrasts should be considered. Too much of one color/contrast creates an imbalance, as do background objects that are more colorful than the main subject. Bright or bold colors and busy patterns attract more attention, so keep these elements in the foreground.

Using image editing to create balance

Most images can be balanced even after the shot has been taken. Most image-editing applications include a cropping function, which removes anything outside of those boundaries. If used properly, a simple crop can fix the balance problems of many photographs.

B
This Asian delight is balanced by placing the main image off-center and slightly off-frame and placing a smaller, unfocused bowl in the background.

C
By adding counters to the larger subject, this image is balanced without detracting from its message.

Framing your images

When you think about framing your images, you might think about a nice walnut frame and some low-reflection glass. But there's another type of frame you can use when shooting your digital images—a natural frame. Don't be deceived by the word *natural*, as a natural frame is actually any object in your scene that can create a frame within your image. Natural frames can be doorways, fences, trees, windows, or any number of other everyday objects, and they can be very useful for adding visual interest and further defining the subject of your image. Including frames in your digital images isn't difficult; in fact, digital cameras make it easy to take advantage of this technique.

The digital advantage when framing

Digital cameras have several advantages over traditional cameras that can help make capturing framed images easier. The following are three advantages:

- The LCD screen lets you not only quickly preview your images, but it can also help evaluate exposure adjustments without you having to wait for film to be developed.

- Many new digital cameras offer articulated LCD screens, so selecting unique viewpoints and capturing that perfect frame is much easier than with a fixed viewfinder.

- Selecting frames can even be done after the fact, as the digital format makes it simple to use an image-editing application to crop your images to perfect frames.

Benefits of natural framing

The use of natural frames in photography is a technique that has been used since the introduction of the medium. Natural frames can:

- Add an intimacy to photography, as the borders around the image provide a "window" effect and allow the viewer a sneak peek into the scene.

- Add ambience to the photograph, as the elements used often better define your scene and offer a sense of place.

A

When using natural frames in your shots, it's important to have a clear subject that isn't overwhelmed by a dominant frame.

- Emphasize your main subject by creating a frame within a frame.

- Help obscure unwanted image details, tighten up your composition, and ensure the visual focus of your shot.

Considering the frame borders

There aren't any unbreakable rules or regulations regarding the use of natural frames, as the subject matter and shot selection are so dependent on the elements available in the scene. However, here are some guidelines to keep in mind when setting up a framed shot:

- In most cases, a frame needs to dominate at least two sides of the image. In fact, partial frames are often more pleasing, as a frame that fully encircles the subject can iso-late your subject and make the frame appear insignificant to the shot. **Figure A** on the previous page shows an image with a strong circular frame but a fairly uninteresting center area. You can see how the purpose of the image is never actually established.

- Most framed shots place the frame in the foreground, as it can be difficult to keep your main subject in focus and present a strong frame in the background. If you have a strong background frame, consider exposing for the frame area and allowing the subject to fall to silhouette for a very interesting effect, as shown in **Figure B**.

- When setting up a frame shot, always keep your main subject in mind. Give your subject some space from the borders of the frame, so it's clearly the main element and doesn't appear confined in the image. However, this may be your intention, so you can see how these guidelines are a good starting point, but not necessarily the rules of the game. You'll also want to eliminate any objects that detract from your frame by selecting a viewpoint that gives the frame an uninterrupted presentation.

Adjusting your camera to the frame

As we mentioned earlier, a digital camera has several advantages when it comes to taking framed shots. Here are

B

If you have a strong background image, you can underexpose your main subject and make your frame more interesting.

Shot at f/5.6

Shot at f/8

C

Your aperture selection helps control depth of field in your shot. When exposing a framed shot, make sure you know which elements you want in focus.

D

If your subject area is much brighter than the rest of the scene, you may have to let your frame fall to darkness to properly expose the shot. As you can see, that isn't necessarily a bad thing.

some simple tips to help you create great-looking frames:

- **Use your LCD screen to preview.** Preview and review your images as you take them so you can easily experiment with different camera and lens settings to get the most from your camera and the framed scene you're attempting to capture.

- **Decide on a point of focus.** As you select your frame and main subject, you must think about what you want in focus. A sharp subject with a blurred frame works well, but a focused frame with a blurry subject can be a challenge. In that situation, the frame becomes the main element, so it must be visually strong enough to carry the image.

  Or, you could decide to keep both the frame and your subject in focus. By controlling your depth of field, you can create the right look for your shot. Small apertures (such as f/8) give you a wide depth of field, so more elements of your scene can be in focus. Larger apertures (such as f/2) give a narrower depth of field and can be useful when trying to blur your frame while keeping your subject in focus. **Figure C** shows an example of the same scene shot at different apertures to illustrate this point.

- **Manipulate exposure levels.** Frames tend to be darker than the subject, as the border area usually takes up the negative space in the foreground of the image. In some shots, the difference in light levels from the frame to the subject can be dramatic, so expose for the subject and let the frame underexpose if necessary, as shown in **Figure D**. In the cases where you want both the frame and your subject to be properly exposed but high contrast is blocking you from finding a useable average exposure, consider taking separate shots (exposing for each element) and then using an image-editing application to combine the images.

- **Cropping to create frames.** Another approach to using natural frames in your images is to use the cropping feature of most image-editing applications to reframe an existing digital image. For example, the image shown in **Figure E** was cropped to emphasize a natural border and eliminate portions of the image that weren't as visually interesting. Cropping to a natural frame can strengthen your image and refocus the viewer on your main subject, but keep in mind that cropping removes image detail. If you crop too much, you may not have enough image information to print at larger sizes. However, if you end up with a stronger image, a few inches here and there won't be missed.

E

By cropping out the dead space on the right and top, we strengthened the shot by emphasizing the natural frame.

The Rule of Thirds

The Rule of Thirds is one of the most widely used rules of photographic composition. By dividing your field of view into thirds horizontally and vertically, you create four points of intersection. Placing your main subject on or near those points of intersection should produce a more visually interesting image, as these are the points where a viewer's eyes naturally rest. If you have secondary subjects, they should also be placed on one of the intersection points.

By using the Rule of Thirds when composing your images, you can lead the viewer's eyes around the photo and avoid having them stop dead on a subject placed in the center.

For example, consider the two shots in **Figure A**. The first shot has the subject dead center and, as a result, the picture isn't that interesting. Simply changing the camera position and reframing the shot to apply the Rule of Thirds creates a more interesting shot.

A

A subject located in the center of the frame leads the viewer's eyes to one spot. By applying the Rules of Thirds and placing the subject at one of the intersection points, you can direct the viewer's eyes around the image.

Conveying a sense of scale in your photographs

Have you ever photographed a stunning landscape and found your final image lacked the impact of the original scene? Or, have you ever tried to capture the overwhelming size of a really huge object and ended up making it look less than impressive? The problem may be that the sense of scale in the shot was never defined, so the viewer has no frame of reference with which to be wowed by your shot. There are many types of shots that can benefit from a sense of scale—from architectural photography to vacation snapshots—but learning how to create and control a sense of scale is part of becoming a better photographer.

A person can help convey scale

One of the most common methods for including a sense of scale in photographs is to include a person in your shot. As an instantly recognizable form, a human figure allows a viewer to gauge the figure's size with the other elements of your scene. This is particularly effective when shooting landscapes, whose vastness often lacks a visual anchor to hold the shot together. As shown in **Figure A**, the small boy fishing not only offers a sense of open space in front of him, but also a sense of the place itself.

However, simply placing a person in the picture can lead to an uninteresting shot. Make sure your person blends with the rest of the shot and avoid placing him dead-center. Let the scenery dominate the shot, and place the person where he can best give the viewer an understanding of the size of the main subject.

Take control of your lens

When conveying a sense of scale, the position of your lens has a tremendous effect on a shot. Whether your lens is in a telephoto or wide-angle position affects the density of the scene, the relationship of objects, the field of view, the depth of field, and other essential photographic details. With most digital cameras, you have a limited range of focal lengths to choose from, but by understanding how your lens settings affect the shot, you can use your digital camera's

A
The human form is invaluable when establishing a sense of scale in your photography.

capabilities to develop scale in images.

Using the wide-angle setting

Setting your camera lens for the widest setting gives you a greater angle of view as well as a greater depth of field. This is especially useful when shooting vast landscapes, where having a wide view combined with a large focal range best conveys the sense of space. The wide depth of field allows you to place smaller elements in the foreground while keeping objects in the distance in focus, as shown in **Figure B**.

Using the telephoto position

When your digital camera is at its maximum telephoto setting, the distance between your foreground and background becomes compressed, and your field of view and depth of field are reduced. This makes creating a sense of scale in large spaces, like a mountain scene, difficult, as the perspective of the scene becomes abstract and the focal range is so narrow it's hard to combine the subject with the scene. However, a telephoto setting can be used to convey scale when the background and foreground subjects are easily identifiable. For example, consider the image shown in **Figure C**. The depth of field is narrow, so the rhinoceros and the area around him are the only areas in focus, but the sweeping mountains and valleys in the background fall to abstraction, making even this large animal seem like a small component of the larger space.

B

The immense size of the snow-capped mountain is further emphasized when a smaller object is captured in the foreground.

C

Since the mountains and valleys in this shot are out of focus, they look even farther away from our central subject, contributing to the sense of scale.

Note: *Lenses in the telephoto setting are subject to a photographic effect known as aerial perspective. In this effect, atmospheric haze causes objects that are farther away to appear lighter in color and tone, which creates the illusion of greater distance.*

Change your viewpoint

One of the most dramatic techniques for conveying a sense of scale is to choose an extreme viewpoint. This works best for relating the height of an object, such as a skyscraper or a redwood tree. To get a shot like the one shown in **Figure D**, set your digital camera for its widest lens setting and shoot from close to the base of the object. The sides of the building bend toward the center, making it look even more imposing.

This is an extreme example, but anytime you shoot up at a subject you make it look larger. Conversely, shooting down on a subject diminishes its appearance. Think about your horizon line, as objects above the horizon are visually emphasized, often making them look larger than they actually are.

D

To create a sense of scale in architectural shots, select an extreme shooting perspective.

Note: *Another way to influence the sense of scale in your photography is to thoughtfully frame shots. Objects appear larger when they fill the frame, so if this is your intention, move in close to take up as much of the frame as possible. If your goal is to make your subject look overwhelmed by the scene, move farther away to allow plenty of space around it.*

Taking better pictures using your flash

The vast majority of digital cameras come with a built-in flash. This is handy because it gives you the opportunity to take pictures where there isn't enough available light, but in certain situations it can hurt your picture more than it helps. While shooting with an onboard flash can be tricky, we'll give you some tips on how you can minimize the negative aspects of using a flash, such as flat light and red eye, and reap the benefits of its convenience.

Understanding flash range

Your camera's flash has a specified range at which it functions correctly. If you look in your camera manual, you'll find a minimum and maximum distance listed. Measurements are meaningless unless you can put them to use in some way, so doing some testing is the best way to truly know your range. For our digital camera, the manual said we had a range from 1 to 14 feet away. While you can judge the 1-foot distance easily, 14 feet can be hard to gauge. As a good rule of thumb, if someone is more than a car length away from you, your onboard flash probably won't be effective.

For most flash shooting, it's better to avoid shooting close subjects whenever possible. Not because your digital camera can't handle the exposure, but because the light coming from the flash is too intense.

By backing away, you can improve the quality of the light hitting your subject and gain a more even illumination. As an alternative to getting in someone's face, back up a few steps and use your camera's telephoto abilities to zoom in to get the framing that you desire.

Avoiding glare

When working with a flash, one thing you definitely want to avoid is a situation that causes lens flare. Because your onboard flash is usually positioned very close to your camera's lens, anything that reflects light sends it right back into the camera lens. The result is flare, as you can see in the image on the left in **Figure A**. Not only does flare ruin an image aesthetically, but it also messes up the camera's ability to take a good meter reading while it's taking the picture. Flare tricks the meter into "thinking" enough light has reached the lens when in fact your image is underexposed.

Since a flash is used so frequently indoors, there are

A

Not only does glare look bad, but it can also throw off your camera's light meter and overexpose the image.

a lot of household items to be mindful of as you take pictures. Anything shiny has the potential to cause problems, but you want to be especially aware of mirrors, pictures with glass mounts, eyeglasses, windows, televisions, and even some shiny appliances, such as refrigerators.

To counteract glare from a flat surface, shoot at an angle to the reflective surface rather than head on. That way, the light from your flash reflects off the surface at an angle away from you rather than directly back at the lens. You can see what a huge difference changing positions made by looking at the image on the right in **Figure A**. Not only is there no glare, but we have a better exposure as well.

Reducing red eye

Another problem with built-in flashes being near the lens is the dreaded red eye effect caused by light bouncing off a subject's retina and back into the lens. This creates the red iris that makes your sweet kids look more like demonic pixies. In the top image of **Figure B**, you can see a typical red eye shot.

Some cameras have flashes that help reduce red eye by firing one or more strobes or pre-flashes before the actual exposure. This causes the pupils to contract and not allow as much light to reach the retina, as shown in the bottom image of **Figure B**. For red eye reduction and the pre-flash to be effective, the person must be looking right at the camera.

Filling in shadows

The most useful aspect of having an onboard flash is using it as a fill flash to lighten dark shadows or backlit subjects. Even bright lighting situations can benefit from a small pop of fill light because bright light usually produces dark shadows somewhere in your scene. Even something as simple as wearing a hat or standing near a tree can throw a subject's face into shadow and make it difficult to capture. In **Figure C** we have just that situation occurring. Although it's a bright day,

nearby trees and the child's hat cause important detail to be obscured in shadow.

Keep in mind that each camera handles fill flash a little differently. There may be an actual setting called Fill Flash or you may simply need to reduce the power of the main flash to its lowest level. Make sure you're at least a few feet away from your subject before firing. The farther away you are, the less impact the fill will have.

Another way to eliminate shadows is to diffuse the light of the flash, which effectively softens any shadows and reduces the intensity of the light. Any diffuse material can be used, such as tissue, wax paper, or light colored cloth. Just make sure you don't block any important parts of your camera, such as the viewfinder or light sensor, when attaching the material. Also, don't block too much of the light or your image might come out too dark or lack overall contrast.

Original Shot
No Flash

Second Shot
Fill Flash

C

Fill flash can help pull details out of dark shadows in your scene.

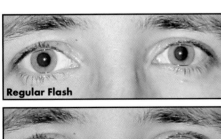

Regular Flash

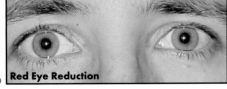

B Red Eye Reduction

In red eye reduction, an extra strobe fires to shrink the pupils and reduce the incidence of red eye.

Using an external flash

Even though your onboard flash is useful, it's very hard to get professional-quality results from a device designed for general use. To get really great flash images, you need to invest in a flash attachment for your camera, as it offers more power and control over your lighting. Also, you need to realize that while shining a small, bright light directly on a subject can provide you with illumination, it doesn't necessarily add the best light to your scene. However, you can bounce the light from your flash attachment off other surfaces to reduce the harshness associated with flash photography and better control the direction and intensity of the light.

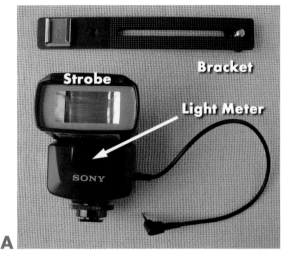

A

A basic flash kit comes with both the flash and a bracket for positioning the unit away from the camera.

Hot or cold?

If your digital camera can support a flash unit, it will have a hot shoe for positioning the flash on the camera body. Although the flash shoe is commonly called a hot shoe, many cameras actually have cold shoes, which are just plastic shoes for flash attachment. They don't actually allow the flash and camera to talk to each other. The hot shoe was the standard method for cameras and flashes to "talk" prior to digital cameras. The hot shoe passes an impulse to the flash telling it when to fire. If you have a hot shoe, you can use third-party flash units by Sunpak, Vivitar, or other companies.

If you have a cold shoe, you'll need to buy the flash from the same company who made your camera so that the flash unit can communicate properly with your camera via a proprietary ACC connector. In reality, even if you have a hot shoe, it's still probably better to buy your flash from your camera's manufacturer just to ensure the most worry-free usage.

Looking at flash anatomy

In **Figure A**, you can see a standard flash setup. This is the HVL-F 1000 that we have for our Sony Cybershot. Most simple flashes like this one cost around $100.

As you can see, it also comes with a small bracket so you can move the flash away from the camera lens to get a little more directional lighting and also avoid red eye. On the flash itself, the strobe head can be pointed toward the subject, toward the ceiling, or any angle in between. It also has a built-in light meter and an ACC connector for linking up with the camera's flash controls. This flash only works on Sony products because of the proprietary connector. Once you attach a flash, it's controlled by your camera's flash settings.

Bouncing light

While the built-in camera flash is convenient, the results aren't fundamentally sound because the quality of the light is so harsh. In photography, creating a good image is all about controlling your light, which is where bouncing light comes into play. Instead of pointing your flash at your subject, you can aim the strobe at the ceiling to bounce the light and get relatively natural-looking light falling on your subject from above. As shown in **Figure B**, we pointed the flash at our scene and just took the shot. Compare it to **Figure C**, where we pointed the flash at the ceiling to bounce the light.

Bouncing the light illuminates the entire ceiling during exposure and basically turns it into a giant diffuser, which results in soft and nearly shadowless lighting. Because flashes have their own light meters, you don't need to make any changes in how you're shooting. It all works automatically, as long as you don't exceed the range of your flash.

Bouncing caveats

When you first start using the bounce technique, it seems like simple magic to make your pictures better. However, there are some problems you'll encounter:

- **You won't always be shooting in a room with 8-foot white ceilings.** If your ceilings are too high, the light becomes too diffused. If they are too brightly colored, you run the risk of introducing color casts into your image.

B

Direct flash creates stark shadows and harsh, frontal lighting.

C

By bouncing the light off the ceiling, you can create a more diffused and natural look to your scene.

- **You also can't efficiently bounce flash in the great outdoors.** And, if you really need a lot of light output, then bouncing is problematic as well because it causes you to lose several stops of light. This may not make much difference in most situations, but the farther away you are from your subject, the more apparent the loss of light power becomes.

D

Bouncing light can create color casts like the added warmth in this image.

- **Bouncing can also induce color casts even from apparently white ceilings.** A lot of paints have metal and brightener components in their makeup, which can generate some surprising results. In **Figure D**, you can see a close-up of our original bounce image from **Figure C**. Even though we bounced the light off a white ceiling, the image has a distinctly warmer color cast. This only took about five seconds to remove in Adobe Photoshop, but it's certainly something to be aware of when shooting.

Adjusting the direction of light

The availability of light in a scene is always important, but of equal significance is the direction that light is coming from. While light intensity influences the exposure levels in your scene, where that light originates also has a dramatic influence on the contrasts, details, and overall presentation of your scene. Light direction defines the shape of your object and creates shadows to add depth. By understanding how light direction affects your scene, you can improve your images and ensure that you set your digital camera properly to avoid underexposed shadow areas or overexposed highlights.

Use the quality of light

The quality of light in a scene is a combination of direction, intensity, and color. When shooting in a studio, you have complete control over these factors, but most of the time you're shooting in natural settings where evaluating the available ambient light is crucial to selecting your camera position and adjusting your exposure settings.

Hard light

When light is coming from a single bright source (such as a light bulb or the sun), it's more directional and is considered a *hard* light. This type of light produces deep shadows, pronounced highlights, and high contrast that can accentuate the texture and shape of your objects. While hard light can obscure detail by blowing out highlights and creating dark shadows, it typically can produce more intense and accurate colors.

Soft light

When light comes from a large, diffused source, it becomes less directional and is considered a *soft* light. As you might expect, soft light produces more subtle shadows, less distinct highlights, and decreased contrast in the scene. Details are preserved, but colors are less intense, yet still accurate. Of course, if a soft light becomes too diffused, such as in fog or haze, colors can become muted, details are obscured, and using light direction as an effect becomes more difficult.

Typical lighting scenarios

Light can arrive from any direction, but generally there are four typical lighting

A

A frontlit subject is very common when using a flash, as it provides an even illumination across the facing surface of your subject.

situations. To demonstrate the influence of light direction, we'll use the hard light coming from a single reflector directed at a bust of our sixteenth president.

Frontlighting

When the light source is coming from behind the camera lens, it falls on the front of your subject, as shown in **Figure A**. This is the best light direction if your goal is to show off the details in your subject. It's also the most common light direction when shooting with a flash, whether it's the built-in flash or an external unit. The problems with frontlighting are also the most common: too bright, harsh highlights and a general "flattening" of the scene due to the lack of shadows, which fall behind the subject. When shooting people, frontlighting causes such undesirable effects as red eye and glare, as well as washed-out colors due to overexposure.

To make frontlighting work, avoid using light that comes in too directly. If you can, try to reposition the camera, the subject, or the light source to provide frontlighting that comes in at an angle. This allows shadows to develop and brings out the textures and details in your subject. You can also find ways to diffuse the typically hard quality of frontlighting to reduce glare or use special flash modes, such as fill flash or red eye reduction to help better illuminate your scene.

Backlighting

While backlighting can be the most dramatic light direction,

B

A backlit subject usually appears as a silhouette, although controlling the exposure between the extreme light and dark areas is difficult.

C

With the light coming from behind, the translucent flower petals stand out, while the center of the flower goes almost to black.

it can also be the most problematic. When extremely bright light comes from behind your subject, it's the shape of your subject that's highly defined while the details are lost. As shown in **Figure B**, the subject becomes a silhouette, and the bright highlights around its edges are difficult to correctly expose. Digital cameras aren't fond of such extreme contrasts, as they can develop *blooming*, where the pixels receive too much light and the digital values are set to pure white. Backlighting is also the main cause of lens flares, which can add noise artifacts, reduce color accuracy, and decrease contrast in your images.

Of course, you can always reposition yourself to eliminate any distracting backlighting, but it can be used effectively if you evaluate the quality of the light in the scene. Backlighting can create stunning shots of a translucent subject, such as the flower shown in **Figure C** on the previous page. The key to this shot is that the backlighting occurred at enough of an angle to allow the exposure to be set for the highlights without losing the detail in the flower. You can also add additional light, such as fill flash to give enough light to brighten up the shadow areas, if necessary.

Sidelighting

This type is the most flexible, as it can come from any angle to the sides of your subject. Sidelighting is perfect for highlighting the texture of your subject and can create a greater sense of depth than frontlighting or backlighting, as shown in **Figure D**. Because the light is coming from one side of your subject, there's a dramatic difference between light and dark with some details lost in the shadows.

The key to using sidelighting is to decide how much contrast you want in your image. If you want to highlight one side of your subject but allow the other to fall into shadow, a hard light coming in at a straight angle does the trick. This setup is often used to create dramatic portraits that emphasize the facial features of the subject. If you want to show the details in the highlight and the shadows of a subject lit from the side, try to increase the angle of the light, make it as diffuse as possible, and expose the midtones of your image. **Figure E** shows how slightly repositioning the light source can cause a big difference in the look of your shot.

D

A light source coming from the side produces interesting contrasts and shadows while emphasizing the details in your shot.

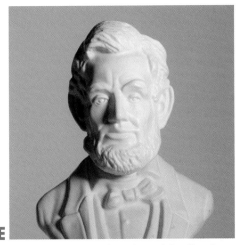

E

By moving the light source slightly forward, the effect of sidelighting is less intense and the contrast is more subtle.

Getting to know your viewfinder's configuration

Did you ever think that your viewfinder might be lying to you? While your digital camera is your photographic eye, what you see in the viewfinder isn't always what your image sensor is capturing. With today's combination of complex optical and electrical components crammed into tiny camera bodies, a wide range of different viewfinder configurations have evolved. By understanding how the viewfinder works in your digital camera, you can make adjustments to your shots and make sure what you see is what you get.

A

While LCD panels have improved dramatically in the past few years, earlier digital camera models featured LCD panels that lacked fast refresh rates and high resolution.

Do you do everything in your LCDs?

Almost every digital camera has an LCD panel. While originally designed as a user interface for viewing and setting camera options, the LCD panel quickly became one of the big advantages over traditional film cameras. Not only could you access menu items, but you could also review your pictures, and of course, use it as a viewfinder. While early digital camera models had LCD panels that were barely passable as viewfinders, as shown in **Figure A**, today's sophisticated models use fast refresh rates, better power management, and more accurate illumination to give the digital photographer a useful way to frame a shot.

The benefits of an LCD panel are pretty obvious, so let's get into some of its drawbacks. The main shortcoming is that LCD panels absolutely devour battery power. This is why most digital camera manufacturers recommend using the optical viewfinder to frame your shots and the LCD panel for accessing the menu and reviewing images. But even this can be a problem on bright, sunny days, when LCD panels can be next to impossible to see. Some manufacturers have come up with low-glare film for the surface of the LCD panel, and there are specially made hoods available to shade your LCD panel, but glare remains a nagging problem.

LCD panels also have trouble with color and contrast accuracy. Since the display is backlit, everything shown in the LCD panel will look slightly brighter and will show more contrast than your actual scene. This can make it hard to manage exposure adjustments while you're shooting.

But how's the view? Well, LCD panels offer a very accurate representation of the information the image sensor receives. Plus, some LCD panels can be angled away from the camera body, so capturing unique viewpoints is much easier. Overall, while the LCD panel suffers from some annoying quirks, it remains one of the most popular and accurate viewfinder options.

Optical viewfinders can be shifty

Another popular method for framing your shot is through an *optical* viewfinder. This is a small window typically set over, or very close to, the lens of the digital camera. It's completely separate from the lens and basically acts as a window to your field of view. Since an optical viewfinder is placed away from the lens, it doesn't represent a completely accurate depiction of what the lens is capturing. As illustrated in **Figure B**, this can lead to a problem called *parallax error*.

An optical viewfinder mimics the view and focal length of the current lens position, but because they aren't in the same place, some offsetting of the image will occur. It's most noticeable when taking close-up shots, but barely discernible on wide-angle scenes. This is why you see target lines when you're looking through your optical viewfinder. As shown in **Figure C**, the manufacturer has placed them there to make it easier to frame your close-up shots. In our opinion, it isn't even worth bothering with the optical viewfinder when framing close-up shots. Use your LCD panel instead to get a much more accurate view of your scene.

B

Parallax error occurs when the viewfinder is placed away from the lens, so what you see is not necessarily what you get.

C

Most optical viewfinders include target lines to help you frame your close-up shots more accurately.

Of course, there are a few more drawbacks to optical viewfinders. They only show between 85 to 90 percent of the actual scene, which explains why the third cousin you so carefully framed out of the shot showed up in the image anyway. Optical viewfinders also don't give you any information regarding color accuracy or contrast, or whether the image is in focus.

Even with these impediments, the optical viewfinder makes for a decent viewing system. It takes absolutely no power and has few to no moving parts. It's easy to follow fast-moving action and it's one of the best choices when shooting in bright conditions, as reflections and glare aren't an issue. Finally, the optical viewfinder is quick and easy to use, which is a benefit for a point-and-click user who doesn't want to mess around with a swiveling LCD panel.

Through the looking glass

Generally used with more expensive cameras, the TTL viewfinder is considered the best type of viewing device. A standard on most SLR (single lens reflex) film cameras, TTL systems are just starting to appear on consumer-level digital cameras. While the complex mechanisms that are used in TTL viewfinders differ greatly, the basic premise is that the light coming in through the lens is diverted into the viewfinder for framing and focusing purposes, as shown in **Figure D**. When you press the shutter button, the light

D

A through-the-lens viewfinder uses optics to divert the incoming light from the lens to the viewfinder.

is redirected into the image sensor for capture.

The main benefit of a TTL viewfinder is that what you see is what you get. When you look through the viewfinder, you're actually looking straight through the lens, so the parallax error isn't a concern. It also consumes no additional battery power and it's very easy to use.

The disadvantages of the TTL system play off its benefits. Depending on the optical system used to divert the light (usually a mirror or prism), only a fraction of the light coming though the lens is actually seen in the viewfinder. This can make it hard to focus or to even see the scene in low-light situations. There's also the possibility for camera vibration when the mirror or prism is moved to redirect the light, increasing the risk of blurry images. Finally, these complex optical systems are expensive to produce and prone to mechanical failure, making them more expensive to purchase and maintain.

Electronic viewfinders

The final type of viewfinder we'll look at is becoming very popular with new digital

Use diopter correction to compensate for eyeglasses

Some digital cameras equipped with optical viewfinders come with a diopter correction. This device allows near- or far-sighted users to avoid wearing their glasses when shooting. Instead, the diopter correction can be used to adjust the viewfinder to match the user's eyesight.

cameras. The *electronic* viewfinder is a tiny, low-powered monitor placed inside the viewfinder. You've seen them before, as this technology is migrating over from video cameras. The electronic viewfinder displays an image that's been subsampled from the image sensor, so again you're looking through the lens. Electronic viewfinders are useful because they don't require as much power as an LCD panel and can perform equally well in bright or low-light situations. An added benefit is the ability to see menu options and camera readings in the viewfinder, making it easy to evaluate a scene and make adjustments.

The drawback to electronic viewfinders is that they're quite small, so seeing detail in your image is next to impossible. Since they're backlit, they also can give a brighter version of the scene like an LCD panel does. However, look for electronic viewfinders to become more prevalent as the technology develops.

Testing your viewfinder

Now that you know the different types of viewfinders, you're aware of the pros and cons of each type. But to truly know what to expect when you frame a shot, you need to test your own camera. It's a simple procedure, and one that works with any type of viewfinder.

Your test subject

To perform a simple test to determine the accuracy of your viewfinder:

1. Place a white 8.5-x-11-inch piece of paper horizontally on the ground, preferably on dark-colored carpet or pavement.

2. Position yourself directly over the paper and look through your viewfinder. Frame your shot so you've lined up the left and right edges of the paper to the view in your viewfinder.

3. Move closer to the page or zoom in to get the shot framed correctly. Don't worry about framing the top and the bottom for now, and don't bother setting the flash or getting the page in focus, as it isn't that important for this example.

4. Take a picture of the piece of paper.

5. Download the file to your computer. The only place to see 100 percent of the image area is on your monitor; so don't even think about using that sneaky LCD panel.

6. Open the file in your favorite image-editing program and take a look.

The envelope, please

The results may surprise you. As shown in **Figure E**, a perfect fit in the viewfinder translated into a lot of extra image information in the image file. We took three shots—two with the optical viewfinder of our digital camera and one using only the LCD panel. The shot taken using the LCD panel as a viewfinder was pretty close, with only a small amount of carpet showing on the left, right and bottom. The two shots taken using the viewfinder were *way* off, with the zoomed shot performing worse than the wide-angle shot. Remember that parallax error is much more evident close up than far away, as our example clearly illustrates. When in doubt, use your LCD panel for the most accurate framing and leave some extra space around the edges of your shot.

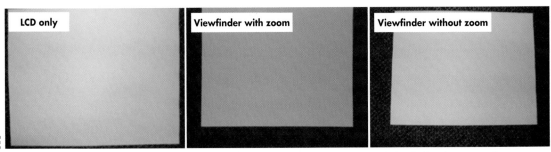

E

The shot taken with the LCD panel was fairly accurate, while the two shots taken with the optical viewfinder displayed severe parallax error.

Using a gray card for proper exposure

A camera's built-in meter allows you to determine the correct exposure for your shots. Many cameras do this automatically and do it well, but it's important to keep in mind that various lighting or subject situations can trick meters into making less-than-ideal exposures. This is when it's handy to have a gray card to act as a midtone reference for your camera's meter, to help you get the best exposure possible. (A *gray card* is a piece of heavy cardboard that reflects 18 percent of the light hitting it—perfect for setting exposure levels.) Once you know how to use a gray card, we're sure you'll find it to be a worthwhile addition to your photo kit.

How light meters work

Light meters are basically averaging devices. When you point your camera at a scene, the camera gathers the tonal information and tries to create a midtone. This works if your scene has a good balance of tones. However, certain situations can trick the meter. That's where the gray card can help because it's essentially an artificial midtone that you can add to your scene to help your meter take a good reading.

As far as tricking a meter goes, an overabundance of white in your scene could cause your meter to tell you to underexpose, while a dark scene could cause you to overexpose—both situations are skewing the average. If you've done much photography in the snow, then you know that snow has a tendency to appear gray because the in-camera meter looks at all that white and tries to balance it to gray.

Types of meters

To use a gray card effectively, you need to have a spot meter built into your camera. Quite a few digital cameras on the market come with more than one metering system. The most common available in-camera meters utilize some type of averaging or matrix metering, which is typically the default on any camera. You may also have a center-weighted meter and a spot meter. Although in-camera spot meters aren't nearly as accurate as handheld spot meters, you can still find them to be effective tools in tricky exposure situations. If you have a spot meter, select it and let's step through a shoot using a gray card.

Metering and shooting

To shoot using a gray card, with your spot meter selected:

1. Place the gray card in the center of your scene, as that's where most spot meters are designed to take their readings.

2. Zoom in on the gray card so it fills the frame.

A

Our automatic exposure looks a little dark. Let's see if the gray card helps.

B

Metering with our gray card increased exposure by one stop.

C

The generic Indoor setting rendered our scene with a much warmer color temperature than it actually appears.

3. Use your camera's exposure lock to capture the right settings without actually taking the shot.

4. Remove the card, refocus on your subject, if necessary, and take the shot. It's that simple. Let's look at our results.

In **Figure A**, we were shooting under low light and our in-camera meter said a shot set at f/4 at 1/15 was okay, but it seemed a little dark to us. When checking it with the gray card, we got the exposure shown in **Figure B**, which is f/4 at 1/10 of a second. With this lighting setup and our scene colors, there was nearly an entire stop of difference in exposure between our average reading and our gray card spot meter reading. As you can see, it made a significant difference in the rendering of the image. It now has improved detail as well as better tonal rendering.

Another thing to keep in mind is that digital cameras are most similar to shooting slide film. They don't have a lot of exposure latitude. In a well-lit scene, you can generally underexpose by one-half or one-third of a stop to get the best results. You can do this most easily using the exposure compensation (EV) feature of your camera. That way you don't have to worry about trying to calculate the right exposure in your head. You can let the camera make the adjustment for you automatically.

Note: Gray cards are handy, cheap, and portable, but there will be times when you don't have them or you can't use them. Green grass is frequently referred to as the poor man's gray card. If you're taking an outdoor shot, take a meter reading of the grass that shares the same lighting as your main subject.

Out of balance

Your gray card has a dual purpose in that it can also help you establish white balance. This is because gray cards are typically white on the other side. So, just flip the card over to set the white balance as well as the exposure.

Most cameras come with lighting presets, but they're generic settings that may be helpful, although not necessarily ideal, for a specific set of lighting conditions. In **Figure C**, you can see our test image shot using the Indoor, or *tungsten*, lighting option on our camera. This image has the same exposure as **Figure B**, but as you can see, the color of the image is quite different. In **Figure B**, we manually set the white balance with the aid of a white card.

To set white balance:

1. Set the white side of the card facing the camera. Zoom in on the card so it fills as much of the frame as possible.

2. Follow your camera manual's instructions for setting white balance. The white balance setting will be retained in memory for the rest of your shoot.

Selecting the correct ISO setting

When digital cameras first hit the consumer market in the 1990s, manufacturers borrowed a bunch of terms from traditional film photography to help potential buyers relate to the new technology. Unfortunately, some of these terms were far from accurate when comparing film exposure to digital capture. One of the greatest offenders is the use of the term ISO to describe a digital camera's sensitivity to light. While the ISO value for film is a straightforward concept, understanding how ISO affects your digital camera can be confusing. Selecting the appropriate ISO setting when shooting with your digital camera is crucial for reducing pixel noise and maintaining image quality.

Understanding ISO

The acronym *ISO* stands for *International Organization of Standards*, a non-governmental collection of worldwide standards agencies that attempts to develop international trade by developing standards. What does this have to do with photography? Well, the ISO has a set of standards for many aspects of photography, the most prevalent of which is the system of using ISO standards to rate film speed. Those of us who still remember film (just kidding) know that you can buy film in a variety of film speeds, such as ISO 100, ISO 200, etc. The lower the number, the less sensitive the film is to light. Therefore, a film rated ISO 800 is much more sensitive to light than an ISO 100 film.

Film manufacturers achieve this light sensitivity by increasing the size of the silver halide grain on the film. The larger the grain, the quicker its reaction time to light. This makes higher ISO films better at capturing action shots, even in low-light situations, because the shutter speed can be fast while still achieving a proper exposure. However, this larger grain size comes at a cost, due to the fact that the grains tend to be much more visible to the naked eye. This "graininess" can be avoided by using films with smaller grains, such as ISO 100 or ISO 200, but since these grains need more time to be exposed to light, the amount of time your shutter is open must increase, opening the door for possible blurry images. Higher ISO ratings require less light, so they allow the shutter to be faster, reducing blurring from camera movement.

The digital side of ISO

Digital cameras follow the same basic idea, but in a completely different way. Since digital cameras don't use film, all ISO adjustments are made on the image sensor. If the camera has been set for a higher ISO setting, the pixels receiving the electronic signal that makes

ISO 100

ISO 200

ISO 400

up the image are amplified, increasing the sensitivity to light. The technical term for this process is called *gain*, and it's defined as the amount of electronic signal amplification taking place on the image sensor. Gain is a much better term for describing the light sensitivity of digital camera sensors, but camera manufacturers continue to equate gain capabilities to ISO settings—presumably to help consumers and professionals alike understand how to make adjustments. So, keep in mind that when using ISO ratings with digital cameras, the number is for reference only.

The range of ISO adjustments depends on your digital camera. Some professional digital cameras offer ISO sensitivity up to a dizzying ISO 3200 and down to a sloth-like ISO 80. The mid-level digital cameras usually give a narrower range of choices, such as ISO 100, ISO 200,

and ISO 400. These correspond to the more consumer-aimed film speeds available at any supermarket. But here's the good part—instead of having to pop in a new roll of film when you want to change film speed or even lugging around multiple cameras with different films loaded, you can change the ISO setting right in the camera, giving you greater control when taking your pictures. **Figure A** shows the difference the ISO setting makes when applied to the same scene.

There are some digital cameras that have a fixed ISO setting. This limits your control over the images, but understanding how the process works can help you make smart decisions when shooting your pictures. By understanding how your camera's ISO setting is affected by your shooting situation, you can compose your shots to get the best possible images.

A

On this sunny day, a setting of ISO 100 was enough to get a good exposure, while ISO 400 overexposed the shot.

B

The danger of using higher ISO settings is the development of noise in your image, as shown in this close-up.

Turn down that noise!

When shooting with a high ISO film, there's always the possibility that the images will look grainy. By the same token, shooting images with a digital camera set to a high ISO creates *noise*. The higher the ISO, the greater the possibility for visible noise in your image. When the pixels are amplified, some of them might take in a little too much information and give either a false reading or "blown out" pixels, as shown in **Figure B**. This noise can occur one pixel at a time, or it can come in patches—digital cameras aren't as predictable as film cameras when determining the effect of a higher ISO. However, digital cameras are most susceptible to noise in low-light and shadow areas, as the sensor tries to compensate for the lack of light by amplifying the signal.

As we mentioned earlier, higher ISO settings tend to display more visible noise. The key is the visible part—some of this noise may not appear until you enlarge and print your image. For that reason, it's important to experiment with your digital camera and see how much or how little noise it produces in certain shooting situations and then gauge the amount of visible noise you're comfortable with.

Note: *Since noise makes images more complex, they require more storage space. Reducing noise in your images allows you to use your storage media more efficiently.*

C

Action shots work best at higher ISO settings, as you can use a fast shutter speed while still getting enough light into the lens.

D

Night shots, like this image of the moon, need longer shutter times and higher ISO settings.

Adjusting ISO settings while shooting

So, how do you use ISO settings to produce better digital images? The secret is in recognizing your shooting situation and constantly making adjustments. Sure, your camera might have an Auto setting that does the work for you, but how can you be sure that your digital camera is making the right decisions?

The first thing to determine is what type of action you're shooting. Action shots require faster ISO settings to *freeze* the action, such as the one shown in **Figure C**, while landscape shots can be taken at much lower settings. The faster the subject, the faster your ISO setting should be.

An equally important factor when choosing an ISO setting is the amount of available light in your scene. When working in a lower-light setting, a slower film speed is required to keep the shutter open longer and let in more light. In the moon shot in **Figure D** on the previous page, we used a higher ISO setting to make the sensor more sensitive to the low-light levels.

Finally, the potential range of shots is important when setting your camera. If you're going to exclusively take action shots, set your ISO setting high and forget about it. If you're going to be at a party indoors where low light and staged group shots will be the norm, set your camera for a lower setting, such as ISO 100. If you plan on shooting a wide range of shots, you'd be best served by selecting either ISO 200 or the Auto setting if it's available.

Choosing an ISO-friendly camera

If maintaining control over your ISO settings is important to you, there are a few options to consider when selecting a digital camera. First, look for a camera with the maximum range of exposure settings, including aperture, variable shutter speed, and, of course, ISO settings. Next, look for a range of ISO settings that fit your shooting style. Just because the new professional digital camera can shoot ISO 3200 doesn't mean you need to plunk down two grand when you won't shoot over ISO 800. Finally, look for a camera that lets you control the amount of in-camera sharpening. Sometimes, though, this feature does more harm than good by emphasizing noise in your image. Turning image sharpening off and adjusting your image in an image-editing program offers the greatest control.

Troubleshooting your noisy digital images

As we mentioned in "Selecting the correct ISO setting," higher ISO settings tend to display more digital noise than digital images taken at lower ISO settings. The fix is to lower this setting to ISO 200 or ISO 100, if possible, which reduces the camera's sensitivity to light. But higher ISO settings aren't always the cause of noise. While avoiding noise might be impossible, here are a few other suspects to consider when trying to quiet your noisy images:

- **Underexposed images.** If an image sensor can't get enough light to capture an accurate reading, it's likely to misinterpret the signal and produce noise. You can fix this by increasing your exposure compensation or your shutter speed.

- **Blue skies.** For very technical reasons, digital cameras and blue skies don't get along. First, the subtle color shifts and large areas of uniform color can cause noise to develop as the sensor tries to reproduce the gentle gradient. Another factor is the infrared filter on most CCD sensors, which tends to increase the sensitivity to the blue end of the spectrum. There isn't much you can do to fix this outside of using an image-editing program, but camera technology is improving every day!

- **Automatic sharpening.** Some cameras let you apply a sharpening filter to your images during capture, which can emphasize noise. Try reducing the amount of sharpening or simply turn off this feature.

- **Shadows.** When a digital camera evaluates a scene, it adjusts the exposure to get the best overall image quality. However, shadows often become noisy, especially when a majority of the scene is bright. Consider using your camera's manual settings or slightly underexposing the shot. You can lighten up the remainder of the image later in an image-editing software.

- **Image compression.** When an image is compressed into a JPEG, there's always a loss of detail. At higher compression rates (lower JPEG quality settings), more noise will develop as the image is broken down into simpler elements, reducing the amount of detail in your image. If this is a concern, shoot with the best possible JPEG quality setting or choose the higher quality TIFF or RAW format if available.

- **Night shots.** Digital cameras don't do well at night. Low light means higher ISO settings, lower shutter speeds, and wider apertures. The more time the image sensor is exposed to light, the greater the possibility that noise will develop. Try to manage your exposure settings wisely and experiment with different configurations to see what works best for your camera.

- **Hot pixels.** Believe it or not, pixels on the image sensor can get too hot—especially if you're taking long exposures, shooting continuous shots, or shooting on a particularly hot day. If you're noticing noise in your images in these situations, try pausing between shots to give the sensor a chance to cool down.

Understanding your lens specifications

Other than the image sensor, there's no component that's more important on your digital camera than the lens. A good lens allows you to get clear, focused shots while offering the flexibility to creatively frame your subjects. Understanding how your lens works allows you to make informed decisions on how to shoot in a variety of situations.

For example, most digital camera lenses have a tough time taking a close-up shot when set for a wide angle. We'll get into why in a moment, but the result in a portrait situation is a flatter, wider face. To resolve this, simply back away from your subject and use the optical zoom on your digital camera to reframe the shot. Now the face will return to its normal proportions, as shown in **Figure A**. By knowing how your lens responds to situations such as these, you can anticipate problems or even use these quirks to your advantage.

35 mm vs. digital

As with most features of digital cameras, comparing them to traditional film photography can be downright confusing. Camera manufacturers usually attempt to assuage this uncertainty by using the 35 mm format as the frame of reference. This is no different with lenses, as most photographers understand what a 24 mm lens or a 100 mm lens can do. However, the calculations for these lens types are based on a 35 mm frame (36 x 24 mm). Most consumer-level image sensors are much smaller, some as small as one-third of an inch. **Figure B** shows the difference between different film and image sensor sizes.

A

The first shot was taken close to the subject's face, causing distortion in the center of the image. By backing up and using the zoom lens to frame the shot, the subject's face returns to the correct proportions.

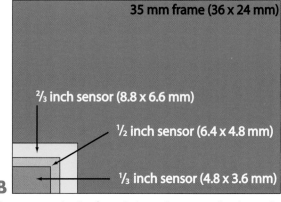

35 mm frame (36 x 24 mm)

²/₃ **inch sensor (8.8 x 6.6 mm)**

¹/₂ **inch sensor (6.4 x 4.8 mm)**

¹/₃ **inch sensor (4.8 x 3.6 mm)**

B

As you can see, the size of even the largest image sensor is only a small fraction of the size of a 35 mm frame.

For example, a typical 4-megapixel ⅔-inch image sensor is only 8.8 x 6.6 mm! And, of course, these sizes vary from manufacturer to manufacturer, making this standard 35 mm "equivalent" a highly variable range. Plus, the high-tech lenses of the new breed of diminutive digital cameras can make a research project out of figuring out what your lens specifications are.

Our recommendation is to consider the manufacturer's lens description to be a working range for your digital camera lens, primarily when it comes to focal length. Let's take a more in-depth look at what's really going on with your lens.

Zooming in

The best place to start when evaluating your lens is its zoom range. Taking a page from video camera makers, digital cameras usually have zoom ratios listed as 2X, 3X, etc. This figure is the range of magnification the lens can cover from its widest angle to its greatest telephoto position. The amount of magnification on digital cameras is usually around 3X, or three times the size of the widest angle. Having a large zoom range gives you the flexibility to take a wide range of shots, from distant objects to close-ups.

Several of the new, higher megapixel cameras are now boasting 6X, 8X, and even 10X zoom ranges, which can add considerable cost to the camera. However, since most digital cameras can't use interchangeable lenses as easily

as a 35 mm setup, having a large zoom range gives you a great shooting range. **Figure C** shows the difference between several popular zoom ranges.

Most digital cameras have two types of zoom: optical and digital. Optical uses the glass in the lens to magnify your scene, while digital zoom uses software inside the camera to enlarge the pixels. This procedure is exactly the same as enlarging an image in your photo editor. However, it's much more destructive to your image, as it just enlarges the pixels on your image sensor. Even though you might have a digital zoom on your camera, avoid it and use your photo editor to make any magnifications beyond the range of your optical zoom.

Note: *Most digital cameras feature Wide and Telephoto buttons to control your zoom range, although some of the newer models are moving back to the familiar zoom ring on the lens housing.*

The tricky world of focal length

The non-technical definition of the *focal length* of a digital camera lens is the distance between the lens surface and the image sensor. The larger the distance, the stronger the magnification factor of the lens. Focal length is measured in millimeters (mm), and as we mentioned, typically rated to a 35 mm equivalent.

Focal length determines the angle of view for your camera. When a camera has a short focal length, it has a wider angle

C

A large zoom range gives you more opportunities to frame your shot.

of view. When a camera has a longer focal length, the field of view is narrower. Focal length is listed as a range of numbers. For example, the Canon PowerShot G2 has a focal length of 35 to 140 mm. This gives it a zoom range of 4X, as 35 mm multiplied by 4 equals 140 mm.

When you increase the focal length of a lens by zooming in, there are a couple of things that happen. First, your depth of field decreases. This makes focusing in on your subject more important, as the focal range is much smaller than a wide angle. Second, zooming in tends to flatten your image. As we mentioned earlier, close-up shots taken at a wide angle tend to emphasize objects in the center of the frame. So, if you're planning to shoot a portrait, you might want to consider placing your tripod a little farther away to get the most flattering representation.

Note: *Ever wonder what the field of view is for your eyes? Since everyone's eyes are different, there isn't an exact number. However, 50 mm is considered a normal lens, or one that provides a field of view close to that of the human eye.*

F-stop on a dime

Ever hear someone refer to a lens as "fast" or "slow"? What they're referring to is the maximum f-stop your lens can support. The higher the f-stop, the better your lens performs in low-light situations and when you want to freeze motion. But wait, you say, aren't most digital cameras notoriously bad for low-light shooting? It's true, digital cameras are known to have problems getting enough light to the sensor when using higher f-stops. But improvements to image sensors and advances in lens technology have allowed digital cameras to feature much faster f-stops. Most digital cameras range from f/2 to f/16, with the lower numbers being "faster." Since adding more f-stops to a camera increases its cost (since the lens must be more complex), most have a very limited range of f-stops. If low-light or action shots are important to you, look for a camera with a fast lens. Higher f-stops produce very narrow depths of field.

Macro-licious

Since digital cameras typically have very wide lenses, it makes it easier for lens manufacturers to add a macro focusing capability, meaning the camera can focus at a very close distance. There are a few things to remember when using the macro mode on your digital camera. Using a flash is discouraged, as you'll be so close to your subject that the bright flash is almost sure to produce hotspots. Also, be aware that a lens in macro mode usually has a very narrow depth of field, so getting your focus right before you take the shot is crucial.

Part 3—Storage and Output Options

One great thing about digital photography is that you're freed from the limited number of exposures offered by traditional photographic film. However, the digital photographer is limited by the capacity of his storage medium. Becoming familiar with storage options and functionality is key to keeping your photos organized and safely stored.

Once you've begun taking digital photographs, you're bound to want to share your images. Since your images are digital, you can share them electronically much more quickly than the traditional film photography development process allows. However, you'll want to take the time to prepare your photos properly for the medium in which you wish to share them.

In this part, we'll show you how to rename your files for better organization, how to select the removable storage medium that will work best for you, how to make smart choices about archiving, and how to make the most of CD-ROM or DVD storage. We'll also discuss considerations and preparation techniques for preparing your images for the Web, email, and online auctions.

Renaming digital camera files

Applications: Adobe Photoshop 7/CS, Adobe Photoshop Elements 2

Digital cameras usually number images sequentially, which has the main benefit of never having two files with the same name. However, does *DSCN5067.jpg* tell you what the image looks like? Or when you took it? There are some digital cameras that allow greater control over the naming of your files as they're being captured, but you're much more likely to rename your files to make some sense out of them once they're downloaded. By knowing what information you want to collect from a filename, you can create a naming convention that makes it easy to find the right shot. And, by thinking ahead, you can save time by renaming large numbers of files at once.

Designing a naming convention

As long as you heed the limitations of your operating system, you can name your image files anything you want. For Microsoft Windows 98/2000/XP users, this means up to 255 characters, except for the following: \, /, :, *, ?, ", <, >, and |. On the Mac, filenames can be up to 31 characters long, and the only limitation is that you can't use a colon (:). Filenames aren't case sensitive for either operating system, but the case is preserved. If you're planning to use these files on the Web, stick with lowercase characters. There are other limitations for the length of a path that includes your filename, but unless you actually use all of the 250 characters in a path, this most likely won't be a problem.

> **Note:** *You also may not be able to use a backslash (\) for a Mac filename, but this is application-specific. It's best to avoid them.*

You must also consider the file extension, such as .jpg. Both Windows and the Mac use fancy OS tricks to hide the extension from view, but you should always include one when renaming a file or designing your naming convention. The standard three-character extension is the most common, although you'll see files with *.tiff* or *.jpeg* from time to time. The file extension helps the OS launch the correct application and allows the application to correctly interpret the file format. Think beyond your current setup and use the three-character extension. It will be around for much longer than your current image-editing application or OS.

What information is important to you?

When designing your naming convention, think about what

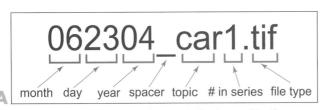

A month day year spacer topic # in series file type

A good naming convention keeps your files organized and easy to identify.

data is going to be the most valuable to you when trying to locate the file. For example, Figure A shows how a naming convention can be used to provide a lot of information in a small space. Using standardized filenames reduces the possibility for errors and keeps your images both nicely organized and easy to locate.

Keeping track of your time

Most naming conventions use some kind of date marker to indicate when the images were taken. This can be any combination of date formats, such as 050104, 20040501, May012004, etc. Determine which aspect of the date is important to you, whether it's just the year or even the exact second the shutter was snapped. A date format places the files in an easy-to-follow order, especially if you place it at the beginning of the filename. Keep in mind that the file-creation date changes whenever the file is saved, so adding a date gives you a reliable method of preserving when the shot was taken, even after it's been edited.

Describing image content

The naming convention discussed earlier satisfies the need to keep images organized sequentially, but it doesn't offer any information about the content of the file. It wouldn't be as useful for files in an image catalog, for example, unless you add some additional descriptive information. Again, select information that will make the file easy to recognize, such

as Family_picnic or Wedding Reception. It might not be realistic to rename every file in your image archive, but renaming groups of images with descriptive names can help you retrieve the specific sets of images more quickly.

Renaming with Microsoft Windows XP

Windows XP offers a method of renaming a group of files. It doesn't offer a ton of control, but it can help you get organized. To select a series of consecutive files to rename:

- Click on the first filename, hold down the [Shift] key, and then click on the last item.

To select nonconsecutive files:

- Hold down the [Ctrl] key and click on each item.

To rename your selection:

1. Right-click on the selection to open the file options menu.

2. Choose Rename from the resulting shortcut menu.

3. Type your new filename and press [Enter]. The selected filenames change to the new name plus a sequential number starting with (1), except for the first file, which just contains the new name. So, if your new name was Party.jpg, your files would be renamed Party.jpg, Party (1).jpg, Party (2).jpg, and so on, as shown in Figure B.

You can also easily add new images to a numbered set. When you have a group of photos you'd like to add to a

Windows XP has useful but limited tools for renaming your digital images.

renamed group, follow these steps:

1. Select the image files as described previously. Right-click on them and choose Rename from the shortcut menu.

2. Enter the series name followed by the *next* number in the sequence surrounded by parentheses. For example, the new name Party (10).jpg would yield consecutive filenames of Party (11).jpg, Party (12).jpg, Party (13).jpg, and so on.

Renaming using Photoshop 7/CS

You can also easily rename files using the File Browser in Photoshop 7/CS. To do so:

1. Place all of the images you want to rename into one folder (which makes it easier) and then launch Photoshop.

2. Select Window ▸ File Browser and use the browsing options to locate your folder.

3. Open your folder and select the images you want to rename.

4. In Photoshop CS, select Automate ▸ Batch Rename

from the File Browser menu to open the associated dialog box. In Photoshop 7, select the File Browser option menu and select Batch Rename.

As shown in **Figure C**, you can rename the files in the same folder or move the renamed files to a new folder. In the File Naming section, you can enter up to six different components to your filename, including automated rules from the dropdown menus next to each box. As you can see, we've set up a naming convention that starts with the date, adds an underscore to separate the date from the rest of the data, a descriptive name, an automated two-digit serial number, and, finally, the file extension. Photoshop gives you an example of your new filename structure, in our case, 040819_oregon01.gif.

Note: *You can also make sure the file is compatible with other operating systems by selecting the Windows, Mac OS (Mac OS 9 in Photoshop 7), and Unix check boxes at the bottom of the dialog box.*

If you name it, you can find it

Giving your image files useful names helps for quick retrieval and easy browsing. When you're working with visual information, adding the appropriate data can help you find what you're looking for and avoid what you aren't. But remember, a naming convention is only useful if you stick to it.

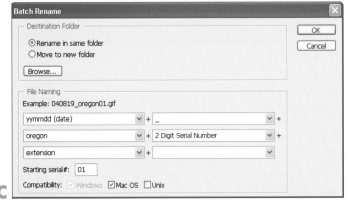

C

Photoshop's Batch Rename feature makes it easy to create a naming structure using a series of dropdown lists.

Portable storage devices

In a typical day, most digital photography enthusiasts can blow through a 64 MB memory card without too much trouble, dumping the images on their computer's hard drive whenever the card fills up. But what happens when you go on vacation and you're away from your computer? Now everything begs to be photographed, and that 64 MB memory card isn't quite meeting your storage needs. Sure, you could buy a larger card (or cards), but even the larger-capacity cards will hold only a portion of the photos you'd like to take, especially if you're shooting at higher resolutions. Or, you might consider carrying a laptop computer everywhere you go, but that adds more weight and liability to your travels.

Many digital photographers are turning to new portable storage devices that allow you to download the contents of your memory card to a large-capacity hard drive without the use of a computer. These gadgets are small, mobile, and easy to use whether you're on vacation or just away from your computer. And, with storage capacities on the rise while prices are dropping, now may be the time to consider getting one for your digital photography setup.

Save time, save money

Even with the price of memory cards falling and capacities rising, purchasing additional memory cards may not be an economical solution. A 256 MB CompactFlash card is still about $60, so getting 1 GB worth of portable storage would cost you over $200. For that price, you could get a 20 GB portable storage device and a handful of card adapters that give you access to all your memory card configurations. With 20 GB at your disposal, you can shoot for days without having to worry about storage space.

Small but effective

While there are a handful of devices on the market, they all work similarly. Each model contains a microprocessor, an operating system, a 2.5-inch hard drive (similar to the smaller drives used in laptops), and a portable power supply. The user interface is usually some kind of LCD screen, which allows you to access the menu controls and image information, but some have full-color LCD screens that allow you to preview your images. You download memory cards via a PCMCIA card slot with a memory card adapter to fit the type of media you're using. When you're ready to dump your pictures from your digital wallet onto your desktop or laptop computer, you can plug in to it using either a USB or FireWire connection.

What to look for

When shopping for a digital wallet, you should take

a number of factors into consideration. Of course, price is always a dominant factor, but let's take a look at some of the operational characteristics you should evaluate when checking out various models:

- **Is it compatible with your current devices?** First and foremost, make sure it can read your type of storage media, either directly or with a card adapter. Since most of these storage devices have an industry-standard PCMCIA card slot, this shouldn't be a problem. However, you may want to avoid models that are specifically designed for a particular type of media so you can continue to use the device if you change media types.

  Also, check that the device works with your computer's operating system. Support for the Mac is still sketchy, but there are models out there. It's equally important to make sure you have the ports available to connect the device to your computer, whether they're FireWire or USB.

- **How much storage do you need?** There are models available from 1 GB to 40 GB, so you should evaluate your shooting needs and buy accordingly. A 3.34 MP sensor produces a compressed JPEG file of about 1 MB, so even a 5 GB device is going to allow you to store about 5,000 im-

ages. Obviously, larger image sensors produce larger files, so think about how much space you'll need and how long you'll go between visits to your desktop/laptop.

- **What about battery life?** Most portable storage devices have internal batteries, but some use external battery packs to extend battery life. Find out how long the device can go between charges, and look for one that provides an AC charger—or even better, a charger that can work from a 12V car outlet. Keep in mind that some power-hungry storage media (IBM Microdrives™ specifically) drain your batteries more quickly than other media types, so check with the manufacturer and look into the battery life for the type you're using.

- **How much do you need to see?** While some kind of LCD panel is standard on portable storage devices, some have a full-color LCD preview that lets you check out your pictures while you're still in the field. Expect to pay a premium for these models, but since most digital photographers have become LCD-dependent, the extra price is worth it. Also, some models allow you to show your images on a television, which can be good for slide shows or just to review the day's shots in the hotel room.

- **What else can it do?** When checking out different models, pay attention to the special features available. Some devices allow you to print directly from the hard drive, either one shot at a time or a group of shots. Others let you reformat your cards on the device, build detailed directory structures, view image histograms, or play movie files taken with your digital camera. Decide which features are important to you, and find the one that fits the bill.

- **Is it cool enough?** Of course, functionality is your main concern, but consider some of the more subjective attributes as well. Try to get your hands on the device and see if you like its size, weight, etc. Are the menus intuitive and easy to follow? Does it seem durable enough to survive out in the field? Do you like the way it looks? These are just big hard drives, but that doesn't mean they can't be attractive as well as functional. And remember, you're going to have to carry it around, so make sure it isn't going to weigh you down.

Note: *When you research these devices, you may notice that some can be shipped without a hard drive. This allows you to install your own 2.5-inch hard drive, making it easier to pick the storage capacity you need for the job. As of this writing, the maximum was 60 GB, but capacities are rising constantly.*

You can take it with you

These portable storage devices are a functional solution for the storage-challenged. Instead of having to buy a bunch of expensive memory cards, you can invest in a storage device with a much larger capacity as well as the flexibility to grow should your storage media change.

Making smart archiving choices

What are you doing with your digital images? If you're like a lot of photographers, you may be having trouble keeping track of them all. As photographers embrace digital capture, most are generating more images than ever before and they all have to be stored somewhere if you want access to them in the future. Storing digital images has become a pressing and complex issue for businesses, libraries, and museums as well as digital camera enthusiasts.

Asset management

First and foremost, your archiving strategy should be developing an organizational system you can stick to. It doesn't do you a lot of good to spend time archiving your images and then not be able to find them. This is where asset management is key. You can create searchable databases that allow you to locate any image you've created. There are several pieces of software that can help you archive your images, many with a particular focus. For example, an asset management system geared toward the medical community is going to have features that the home user would never use—so do your homework when deciding which to use.

Technology changes

The real problem with archiving digital images is the inevitable onslaught of technology changes. If your images were stored on 5.25-inch floppy disks, you can imagine the difficulty you'd have trying to open them now. Because technology is constantly changing, in as few as 25 years, you could lose access to your images if you don't have a sound migration strategy in mind. How many computers now can read the SyQuest® disks of seven years ago, let alone the punch cards of 30 years ago?

You have no control over the obsolescence of various hardware and software. As times change, you need to move your digital images from one type of media to the next standard. For an individual this might not be a big deal, but for a corporation this could be incredibly time-consuming as well as expensive. Be sure to make plans about how you're going to systematically update your media, and choose formats that are widely used. This gives you a better chance of retrieving your images if your equipment doesn't stand the test of time. Just ask anyone who still has files on a Bernoulli! Also, choose non-proprietary file formats like TIFF or JPEG.

A

Compressing an image to the same file size yields much better results with JPEG 2000 than with the original JPEG format.

While Adobe Photoshop may be around forever, do you want to take the chance and save everything in the PSD format? Go with a file format that can be opened in many applications.

Choosing your media

Your choice of media is of paramount importance for reasons of longevity and future compatibility. For the most part, CD-R disks are the most practical and stable choice for storing digital images. CD-RW disks aren't a good option because of their poor stability.

However, there are problems with CD-R disks as well. Quality control varies widely and they can delaminate or fail in other ways, which usually occurs rather suddenly. Because of this, it's a good idea to have multiple copies of important files. Store one set of images in one location, such as your business or safety deposit box, and another in your home in a fireproof safe.

CD-R quality

There's a lot of debate about the quality of various types of CD-R disks due to their dye color. Several studies concluded that cheap, store-brand CD-R disks don't last as long as higher-quality name brand CD-R disks. It's very much a case of getting what you pay for. A few companies are also making medical grade CD-R disks, which cost considerably more than standard ones, but are supposedly guaranteed for 100 years.

Burn time

Another factor is that the burn speed of the CD-R can affect its quality. A CD is generally more error free with a slower burn speed. This is true even with CDs that are rated to 12x. They show more errors when burned at that speed than when they're burned at 4x. A 4x burn is considered to be cleaner and won't suffer as many problems as the disk degrades over time. Don't be tempted to go slow on the burn times either. 1x burn times have been known to have problems as well, especially when using CDs rated for higher burn times.

Media storage environment

As when storing important photos and negatives, CDs should be kept in a cool, dry environment. Keep sun exposure and humidity exposure to a minimum. The combination of heat and high humidity is the worst scenario for a CD. Ideal recommendations are for a normal office environment with low humidity. Some types of CD-R disks are more susceptible than others, but there's little conclusive information about which types are better. With important data, it's better to be safe than sorry. As with most things, improper handling does more damage than anything else does. A single scratch can make data impossible to read.

File format compatibility

File format is another important decision when archiving images. You'll want to choose something that's read by many applications. With new compression algorithms, such as JPEG 2000, you can have high-quality images stored in less space. You can store your images in many different file formats, but no single software application reads every possible file format. Who knows what software will be like 10 years from now? The JPEG coalition has updated the JPEG format to make it a better compressor as well as more universal and less destructive to image data. It can also contain different color spaces, ICC profiles, and even metadata to make images easier to access with asset management software.

You may think you know all about JPEGs, but JPEG 2000 is a completely different animal. Instead of using the DCT compression that caused those block-like artifacts, JPEG 2000 uses wavelet compression. You can really see the difference in the comparison of the two technologies in Figure A which shows the same image compressed to the same file size with different algorithms.

JPEG 2000 offers both lossy and lossless compression. The lossless compression does a great job—in one of our tests, we losslessly compressed a 14 MB TIFF image into a 5 MB JPEG 2000 file. With this kind of compression, you can get many more images onto a disk with no quality loss.

No more shoe boxes

Keeping track of your images is never fun, but you'll probably be sorry if it's something that you neglect. Storing digital images is important for you and your business. Establishing good practices now and choosing the right storage materials can make the process easier for you now as well as in the future.

Recordable DVDs

With ever-increasing pixel counts comes ever-increasing file size. Recordable CDs remain the most popular and cost-effective storage media for digital images, but the ballooning size of some image archives is causing digital photographers to look for a larger-capacity solution. With our Zip disks filled and the stacks of CD-Rs piling up, recording to the high-capacity DVD is looking better and better. With a storage capacity of 4.7 GB, a recordable DVD can store as much data as seven recordable CDs, and then some. But switching to the DVD format shouldn't be taken lightly, as a format controversy is brewing for this emerging technology that might make you think twice.

DVD basics

The DVD (Digital Versatile Disc) format you're probably most familiar with is technically called DVD Video. These are the discs that contain your favorite movies and play through your set-top DVD player or the DVD drive on your computer. While most DVD Video discs are single-sided, some are double-sided and offer twice the capacity. The big benefit of the DVD Video format is its compatibility with a vast majority of the DVD players on the market. So, buying a DVD player is basically a no-brainer if you just want to play your favorite movies, as the DVD Video format is so standardized.

Note: DVD-ROM is the same thing as DVD Video; however, the DVD-ROM format has been further optimized to work with computer DVD drives.

Recordable DVDs aren't so simple. Since their introduction to the home user only a few years ago, companies have been battling it out over which recordable DVD format is best. Think of it as the VHS versus Beta of the new millennium—and a debate that most likely will be decided by the choices consumers make in the coming years.

Fluctuating formats

As you'll see, the big problem with the various recordable DVD formats is that they have very similar names and accomplish essentially the same thing. For example, all the DVD formats we'll examine have 4.7 GB storage capacities, are the size of a regular CD, and can store data, images, or movies. This makes the selection process a little simpler for digital photographers who just want to store large quantities of data that can be retrieved on a computer, as almost any choice will do. But if you want to do more with your DVDs, such as record movies, make slide shows for your television, or any of the other things DVDs can do, you'll need to understand how the formats differ before you can make an intelligent decision.

- **DVD-RAM.** This format was the first of the recordable DVD formats, but lately it has become the least popular consumer option. DVD-RAM discs could be recorded and erased repeatedly (up to 100,000 times per disc), which is useful for users who need to save and update large files, such as databases or image files. The RAM portion of the title isn't just marketing—DVD-RAM discs use random access memory to quickly find and retrieve data, just like a standard hard drive.

  The drawback to DVD-RAM discs is that they only work with computer DVD drives and can't play on set-top DVD players. Plus, some DVD-RAM discs (Type I) were contained in archaic-looking cartridges to protect them from dust and scratches, making it difficult to share the discs with other users. However, DVD-RAM remains popular with DVD purists.

- **DVD-R.** Just like CD-R, this format allows the user to record only once. DVD-R discs write at 2x, which roughly translates to 18x in CD-R terms. This format is quite compatible with both set-top DVD players and computer DVD drives, but is quickly being overshadowed by the rewritable formats, and with good reason. With a storage size in the gigabytes, it's unlikely that you'll be burning such large disks on a regular basis. By utilizing a rewritable DVD, you have the flexibility to write smaller chunks of data on demand.

- **DVD-RW.** The key to this rewritable format is the dash (-). DVD-RW discs can only write at 1x (2x if writing in DVD-R mode) and are aimed primarily at the consumer market. DVD-RW doesn't have the error checking and random access capabilities of the original rewritable DVD format, DVD-RAM, but it's highly compatible with all kinds of DVD players. It also offers a shorter lifespan of around 1,000 rewrites. However, DVD-RW discs are much cheaper than DVD-RAM discs and perform admirably in accuracy and efficiency tests.

- **DVD+RW (and DVD+R).** Notice the plus sign in this one? Well, the plus means added speed, as the DVD+RW format can write at 2.4x, which is 140 percent faster than DVD-RW. This speed comes at a price, as DVD+RW discs are much less compatible with set-top boxes and more expensively priced. Proponents of this format (Sony™, Philips™, and Yamaha™ among them) are quick to point out that most DVD+RW drives are able to write to the DVD+R format, which is compatible with most of the newer DVD players. DVD+RW also has some additional benefits, such as quick disc formatting and on-disc editing.

Which one is for you?

At this point, the recordable DVD standard continues to evolve, but the battle seems to be between DVD-RW and DVD+RW. The DVD Forum (www.dvdforum.com), the defining body of DVD format specifications, recognizes DVD-R, DVD-RAM, and DVD-RW as valid DVD format choices. The DVD+RW alliance (www.dvdrw.com) has some major players pushing their format. Sony, perhaps hedging their bets on all formats, produces a drive for all of the formats, including some drives that can record to both DVD-RW and DVD+RW.

DVD for the digital photographer

For the digital photographer who wants to create archives of his images on DVD, the DVD-R, DVD-RW, or DVD+RW formats will work fine. Since there's little need for compatibility with set-top DVD players, it might seem a moot point to worry about formats for data storage. However, make sure you think ahead when making your format choice. Today's DVD players can play CD-Rs filled with MP3s and VCD discs filled with home videos—features that weren't even imaginable a few years ago. Will the next generation of DVD players also be able to play back your image archive, perhaps on a high-definition television at full resolution?

Decisions, decisions

Consider that your DVD burner shouldn't be a one-trick pony. You'll want to be able to burn your digital movies and play those back on your television, right? The best and only option for digital photographers, at this time, seems to be DVD-R. The DVD-R format is highly compatible, less expensive than the rewritable options, and more stable for long-term storage (in the decades). However, the DVD+R/RW format is quickly gaining ground and seems to be the format used by most computer manufacturers. Unfortunately, it comes down to doing your research and taking the plunge one way or another.

DiViDed

The DVD format has many benefits, but some important compatibility issues need to be resolved before the format fully takes off. If you just have to have it, consider how you'll use it and keep in mind that you just might have to upgrade in a couple of years. If storing your digital images is the only task your DVD burner will handle, any DVD format will perform well and get the job done.

External hard drives

Ever since the very beginnings of photography, image archiving has been a matter of concern. Not only can environmental factors like moisture and humidity destroy prints and negatives, but these photographic records are also prone to physical damage, such as scratching or tearing. The digital photographer doesn't have to worry much about scratching a digital file, but the need to safely archive your images may be even more important. You might lose a single negative to a scratch, but a crashed hard drive can take thousands of images along with it.

Keeping a backup archive of your images is crucial to ensuring their safety. Many digital photographers use CD-Rs and DVD-Rs to hold their image archives, but questions on the long-term stability of these formats and the limited storage capacities have caused some to turn to a larger storage option. As the size of a single image archive can balloon into the tens of gigabytes, external hard drives are increasingly becoming the preferred storage devices for digital photographers, and we'll tell you why they're worth considering.

Technical details of external hard drives

External hard drives range from a considerable 20 GB to a whopping 500 GB, with capacities increasing all the time. While storage capacity is probably the first feature to consider, there are other features that make some external drives work better than others. When comparing your options, check the drive's rotation speed. Like a car's engine, rotation speed is measured in rotations per minute (RPM), with speeds typically 5,400 RPM, 7,200 RPM, 10,000 RPM, and 15,000 RPM. The faster the rotational speed, the faster the drive can find saved data. Faster also means more expensive, so we recommend looking at the 7,200 RPM models as a good balance of speed and value.

Connection type

The next feature to check out is the connection type. Most external hard drives offer USB 2.0, FireWire, or both. You'll be able to find the occasional SCSI connection out there, but these drives are becoming less common as the other types take over the market. We like the flexibility that the combo drives offer, but if you're going for pure speed, USB 2.0 (up to 480mb/sec) currently is faster than the standard FireWire connection (up to 400mb/sec). Newer FireWire connections offer higher rates (800mb/sec), but both flavors of FireWire are much less common than USB. Another benefit of USB 2.0 is it can be used with an older USB 1.1 connection, although at a drastically reduced speed (12mb/sec). One good thing about both types of connections—they work equally well on the Mac and in Windows.

Drive format

The format of the drive is another consideration. Most external hard drives aren't formatted, so you'll have to format the drive before you use it. You have two choices: FAT32 or NTFS. Without getting too technical, professional archivists recommend NTFS, as it offers the best performance, stability, and security features. However, FAT32 offers faster operation and it's easier to recover lost files should the drive crash. It's a tough decision, so consult your user's manual as well as the external hard drive manufacturer's Web site to figure out which format is right for your workflow. For the record, the drive we use was preformatted with FAT32, and so far we've been satisfied with its performance.

Archiving on an external hard drive

Once your drive is connected and ready to use, take a moment to consider how your files will be arranged on the disk. The archiving technique that makes sense to one person can be completely befuddling to another, so it's hard to make an overall recommendation. However, a popular archival scheme is as simple as a folder for each year that contains separate folders for each month and then folders named with the date of each download session. For example, 2004/February/020104/image.jpg is a typical path in this type of archival system.

This type of date format works for some photographers, while others prefer breaking up their images into categories, such as birthdays or holidays. Whatever you choose, make sure it's consistent. Choose one format for your image archive and stick to it when you copy files to your external hard drive. Doing so allows you to find images more quickly and makes it easier to tell if your archive is up to date.

Preserving your archive

External hard drives are delicate instruments, so you must take care of them as you would your digital camera. Remember that any hard drive can get hot, so place your external hard drive in a well-ventilated spot when in use. When in storage or being transported, properly insulate the drive using padding or an external case that can protect it from any bumps, bruises, and the occasional raindrop.

From there, consider where you'll be storing the drive for the long term. It's always a good idea to have one backup of your files in another location (should disaster strike). Our strategy is to keep one main image archive on a local drive for easy access, a backup of that archive on our external drive, and then a set of CD-Rs or DVD-Rs stored offsite.

Sound like overkill? During our research, we came across one archivist's recommendation that in addition to a separate set of removable media (CD/DVD), you must have one external hard drive for everyday backups as well as a master external drive stored in either a bank vault or a fireproof/waterproof safe that's kept in a freezer. What's next, an armed guard? It comes down to whatever protection makes you comfortable—go to whatever extent you need to, to make sure your images are safe.

Prepping images for the Web

Applications: Adobe Photoshop 7/CS, Adobe Photoshop Elements 2

One of the big advantages to shooting pictures with a digital camera is that you can have your image up on the Web mere seconds after taking it. This immediacy allows us to share our images quickly, but the ease of posting images on the Web has led to an epidemic of bloated file sizes and poor optimization choices. Taking the time to prep your images before posting to the Web doesn't have to be a technical nightmare or take a lot of time. Instead, by considering your audience and planning your presentation, you can display efficient, attractive images that won't break the bandwidth.

post them on the Web. By taking another look at your images, you have a chance to make a final evaluation on composition, color quality, and optimization settings. This way you can make sure your images are perfect before you release them to the world. This may seem a little labor-intensive, but remember that images make a greater and more immediate impact on your viewers than the text and graphics on your Web page. By presenting the best possible images, you help viewers have a positive experience when visiting your site. Let's explore how you can best impact your viewers.

Why not just throw them up there?

Sure, you could just dump your images onto your computer, slap them on an HTML page, and upload away. However, you risk alienating your audience and reduce the chance that they'll enjoy your pictures. Poor presentation, slow download time, inappropriate file format, and poor image quality are the main offenders when posting your digital images on the Web. Any of those problems can make any Web photo gallery quite ineffective.

But there's a bigger reason to take the time to properly prepare your images before you

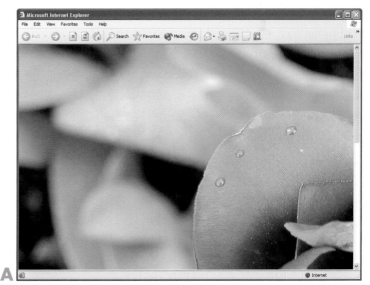

A

Make your images more effective by eliminating the annoying need to have to scroll within a browser to see the entire image.

Know your audience

Creating the optimal viewing experience for your Web images isn't difficult if you take the time to consider how the images are going to be viewed. The equipment used for Web browsing is hardly standardized, so finding a common middle ground when it comes to file size and dimensions will allow your images to be viewed effectively on many different computer systems.

Resize your image

One of the greatest Web sins that you can commit is neglecting to resize your images when you post them. Nothing is more annoying than having to use scroll bars to reveal an entire image, as shown in **Figure A** on the previous page. By resizing your images to an efficient size, you should be able to reach the widest audience possible.

Not everyone has a 21-inch high-resolution monitor; in fact, the standard is just starting to creep up to 17 inches. But monitor size isn't as important as screen resolution, which ultimately decides how large your Web images will be onscreen. Most Web designers plan for a screen resolution of 800 x 600 pixels, although some still stick to the old-school 640 x 480. When it comes to resizing your digital images, a combination of these two figures works best. Plan for a Web page of 800 x 600, but keep your images under 640 x 480. This helps ensure that the images fit onscreen and those pesky scroll bars are kept at bay.

Keep in mind that 640 x 480 is the largest you should make your image—at 72 dpi, this size translates to about 8 x 6 inches. While having big images like this is certainly desirable, you'll want to keep your images as small as possible to reduce overall file size. Even at a moderate compression, a 640 x 480 image at 72 dpi saved as a JPEG takes up 60 K. One image this size might not be a problem, but several of them will choke all but the highest bandwidth.

Reduce file size

Knowing what type of Internet connection will be used to download your images is just as important as knowing what type of monitor your images will be viewed on. While the broadband revolution continues, a vast majority of Internet users use a dial-up modem to gain access. Just as the average monitor size has crept up recently, so has the common denominator number for modems. **Table A** shows some typical download times based on Internet connection.

Most Web designers plan for a 56 K modem (up from the former standard of 28.8 K) and optimize their images for a download time of three to five seconds. Any more than that and your audience might click away for faster-loading entertainment. Decreasing your file size is a matter of reducing your image dimensions and using compression to optimize your file. We'll get more into image optimization later on.

Table A: *Download time for a 50 K JPEG file*

Connection	Download time
28.8 K	14.2 seconds
56.6 K	7.3 seconds
DSL	0.8 seconds
Cable	0.4 seconds
T1	0.2 seconds
T3	0.009 seconds

Plan your presentation

One aspect of image presentation on the Web that's often overlooked is how the image is arranged on the page. If you opened a JPEG image in a browser, the image would look fine, but it would be shoved into the upper-left corner. Think of the Web page as a frame and position your image with a good amount of space and complementary background colors. You can easily do this using your Web-editing software, and it should take about the same amount of time as placing the image in an HTML page.

For example, we always use a white background. Just like a white matte board accentuates a framed image, the white background of the browser contrasts against the image and allows it to stand out. We've also seen tasteful uses of black backgrounds, but try to use this technique only with images that are very light. Other colors may work on an image-to-image basis, but sticking with standard white gives your viewer a consistent viewing environment.

We also center the image on the page each time. This keeps the image right in front of your viewer and provides an even border around it. If you're integrating your image with text, make sure you place the image in a logical spot so neither element detracts from the other.

Finally, we add a 1-point black border around each image. This is a subtle effect, but it helps to frame the image and keeps lighter areas of the image from washing out into the white background. You could definitely experiment with thicker borders, but don't overdo it. **Figure B** shows our setup as compared to simply opening the original image in a browser.

Note: Another good practice is to add an <alt> tag to your images. This gives a text description of the image for those who can't view images or have turned off that function—you might just get them to turn it back on!

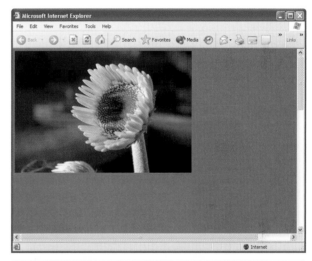

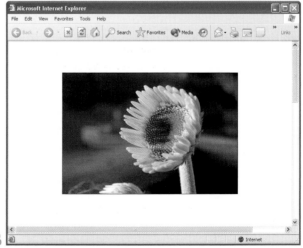

B

By taking the time to properly present your images, you give the audience a better opportunity to enjoy your work. Here, a white background and centered image do wonders for this shot.

Optimizing your images

When optimizing your images, there are two approaches. You could go out and get a degree in digital imaging or you could do what looks good to you. But remember, you're the toughest critic of your own work, so if it looks good to you, it will probably look good to everyone else. There's no need to concern yourself too much with the theory of image compression. Of course, this stuff is important, but use the tools available and your critical eye to optimize your images to the utmost.

Selecting a file format

When we say selecting, it doesn't mean you have a lot of options. In fact, the only good choice when creating continuous tone digital images for the Web is JPEG. There are some techniques that you can use to turn digital images into reasonable GIFs, but the savings in file size are greatly compromised by the decrease in image quality. **Figure C** shows an image saved in both formats. The JPEG format offers user-selectable and variable compression rates, so you can choose how much your file is compressed. Plus, you can add features such as ICC color profiles, image blurring to smooth out sharp pixels, or even create a progressive JPEG, which displays a low-resolution version of your image while the higher resolution version loads.

Optimizing for better quality

We use Photoshop and Elements to optimize our images, but you can use any image-editing application that allows you to change the compression rate on a JPEG. We aren't going to worry about the "extras" you can do with JPEGs; instead, we'll concern ourselves with getting a good-looking image, altering only the compression rates.

To optimize an image, use the following steps:

1. Open your image and make any necessary color and cropping adjustments.

2. Select Image ▸ Image Size (Image ▸ Resize ▸ Image Size in Elements) so you can resize your image to be Web-friendly. Our original shot was taken with a 3 MP camera, so

C
Continuous tone images taken from digital cameras should be posted in JPEG format. GIFs tend to cause banding and a distracting dithering of colors.

we had a lot of image information we didn't need for the Web. Even after cropping it, we had an image dimension of 14.2 x 9.4 inches at 72 dpi. Luckily, this works out to be 4 x 6 inches, or 432 x 289 pixels, which fits into our target image size perfectly.

3. Resize your own image to reduce it to a manageable size.

4. Click OK when you've finished to apply the new image size.

5. Select File ▸ Save For Web to open the Save For Web dialog box.

6. Click on the 2-Up tab above your image so you can view your optimized and original images at the same time, as shown in **Figure D**.

7. Choose JPEG from the Optimized File Format dropdown list and move the Quality setting to 100%. It's always a good idea to start at the top and work your way down—you get a better idea of how image quality degrades.

How much you compress is largely dependent on the content of your image. Large areas of solid color compress better than details, and light areas take up less space than black—so you really have to go on a picture-by-picture basis. Try starting at 100% and decreasing in 10% increments until you

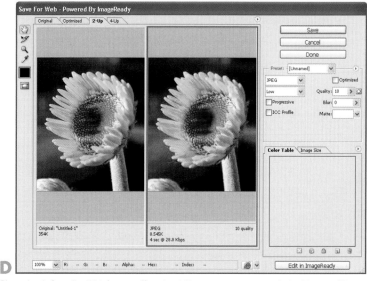

D

Photoshop's Save For Web feature offers the ability to compare your optimized image with the original.

find a good compression rate. Then, move up or down in 1% increments to fine-tune it. The difference in file size between an 88% setting and an 84% setting can be significant, so take the time to fine-tune.

Our image went down to 65% before we started to notice some distracting artifacts. This image's simple background responded well to compression, but the edges of the flower petals had enough detail that visible pixelation occurred once we compressed it further. However, we reduced the file from 123 K to 25 K, which equates to a download time of three to four seconds on a 56.6 K modem. Not bad, especially considering the dimensions of the image. Click OK, name your image, and save it to your hard drive.

Emailing digital images

Email has made sending digital images through the Web a convenient method of sharing pictures. While simply attaching an image to an email and sending it couldn't be easier, you should always prepare your digital images properly before sending to make sure your intended viewer can enjoy them without difficulty. By optimizing the dimensions and file size of your image while following some email etiquette, you can make the process as effortless and enjoyable as possible.

Step 1: Resize your image

The first step when prepping an image for email is to resize it. Many other variables, such as file size, fall into place once you reduce the size of the image. As shown in **Figure A**, most images sent via email appear after the body of the email, or open in a separate window when clicked on. By keeping the image dimensions smaller than the screen size, you can avoid forcing the viewer to scroll. Instead, your image will be shown in its entirety, and your recipient can see the whole image instantly. Reducing the dimensions of the image also has the added benefit of reducing file size, which allows the image to load more quickly.

If you know the dimensions of your recipient's computer monitor, you can always target those attributes. However, most of the time you won't know, or you'll want to send the image to multiple recipients with different setups. The best policy is to resize the image to a reasonable dimension for all monitors. Most Web designers plan on a lowest common denominator space of 640 pixels by 480 pixels when making a Web site, but this would be overkill for a single image (8.8 x 6.6 inches). We've always had success sizing our images to 5 inches wide (360 pixels) and letting the height display proportionately. This offers a nicely sized image that won't need to be scrolled, even on the smallest monitor.

You'll also want to make sure that your resolution is set for 72 dpi. While some monitors display at higher resolutions, a vast majority use the 72 dpi standard. If you save for a higher resolution, the browser or email application in which your image is viewed is going to display the image at 72 dpi anyway,

A

Make your image small enough to fit on the recipient's screen without having to scroll.

interpolating the excessive resolution by increasing the dimensions of the file. This is a classic case of jumbo-sized images that require scrolling, so make sure you save your images at 72 dpi and your images will display as you planned.

You'll also want to ensure that your image is in the RGB color mode. This shouldn't be too much of a worry, as most digital cameras save to an RGB format. However, if you're shooting in the RAW file format, make sure you convert the image to RGB before saving. Images saved in other color modes won't display correctly in most email applications. They can be downloaded by the recipients and opened in an image-editing application, but again, your goal is to make it as easy as possible for them to enjoy your image.

Note: *If your viewers want a higher-resolution image for printing, let them request it. Sending the high-resolution file to every recipient will waste time and fill up their email accounts.*

Step 2: Make image adjustments

The next step when prepping your image is to make image adjustments, such as color balance, contrast, and saturation. There are differing schools of thought on when you should do your image editing—before or after you resize? If you select before, you have more image information and resolution to work with, but you might have to readjust the image once it's resized. As for making

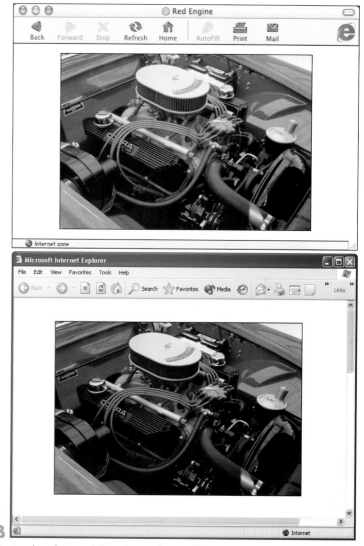

B

Due to color palette restrictions, the same image will look slightly different on the Windows and Macintosh operating systems.

adjustments after you resize, you'll only have to make one adjustment, but you're working with less image information, so fine-tuning the details might be more difficult. We usually like to make our image-editing adjustments before we resize and make smaller adjustments after. It might take a little extra time, but it generally results in a better-looking image.

C

The middle image gives us the same image quality as the first at half the file size, but the last image shows what can happen if you push your compression too far.

One of the adjustments we typically make after resizing an image is to sharpen it slightly. When an image is resized, edges and lines become fuzzy due to the interpolation and the image can look "soft." By sharpening a bit, you can make your images look crisp and allow details to stand out.

Note: Due to the different color palettes of the operating systems, an image viewed in Windows looks slightly darker than the same image viewed on a Mac, as shown in Figure B *on the previous page.*

Step 3: Save your image

Now that your image is properly sized and adjusted, it's time to save this version to your hard drive. *Never* save over your original image! Always save the email version as a new file and preferably in another directory. We've seen too many people save over the high-resolution version of their image by mistake. While they can still view the image, you can forget about making decent prints from the low-resolution version. We keep a separate folder called *Email Images* in which we save all of our prepped images. Not only does it decrease the risk of writing over the original, but

it also keeps all of our edited images together for easy access.

Naming your image

When saving your image, it's best to follow some simple naming conventions. Keep your filenames simple and descriptive. Avoid long titles with spaces, such as *Here's a picture for you.jpg*. While your Windows machine may not have trouble with it, your friend with the iMac might not be able to open the file.

The best policy is to follow the old 8.3 naming convention, that is, eight characters followed by a three-character file extension. Our title is much better as *pic4U.jpg* and will give your users less trouble. You can make your title longer than eight characters, but avoid using spaces and special characters, such as asterisks and dollar signs.

Optimizing your image

The best file format for emailing images is the JPEG format. This format is widely accepted, compresses well, and maintains accurate colors. The key to using the JPEG format to its greatest potential is to minimize the file size by compressing the image. The amount of compression

Things to keep in mind:

- ❏ Don't send hi-res images unless the recipient requests it.
- ❏ Images appear darker in Windows than on a Mac.
- ❏ Don't compress too much—your image quality depends on it.
- ❏ A suitable image size is 5 inches wide (or 360 pixels) with a proportionate height.

is up to you, but be careful. As shown in **Figure C**, too much compression can degrade your image quality.

Note: *If you're unsure that your image will look okay, test it out by emailing it to yourself. It isn't a scientifically proven process, but at least you'll know that the file is valid.*

To group or not to group?

When sending multiple images, it's best to only send a few at a time. Many email applications can receive new messages in the background, so your recipient can view the first group while the others are being downloaded. Some Internet service providers (ISPs) set limits on the maximum size of an email, so sending a few at a time will help your images arrive safely. This size limitation varies greatly, but keeping the total file size of your image group below 1 MB usually does the trick.

Follow up after sending

When composing your email, you may want to ask the recipient to let you know if he had any trouble opening your digital images. By understanding your audience's preferences, you can find out how to better prepare your images to suit their needs.

Before you email it:

- ❑ Resize the image
- ❑ Make image adjustments
- ❑ Save the image
  - o Name it
  - o Optimize it

Quality images for online auctions

Looking to sell an item in an online auction? If you're serious about selling, you'll need a quality image to accompany your text description on the auction site. An image is a crucial selling tool—not only will it attract buyers, but it will also let them know exactly what they're bidding on. Digital cameras are perfect for shooting online auction items, and getting a great shot is a matter of some simple photographic techniques.

The importance of good photography

A good photo is key when using an online auction service. Since your goal is to drive the price up as high as possible, you want to make your item look as appealing as you can and differentiate it from similar items that are competing for the buyer's attention. Since all you have to work with is your written description and your images, think of your images as your product display and your description as your salesperson.

A high-quality image also gives you credibility as a seller. If you have a blurry, poorly lit image, the assumption can be made that you'll be equally sloppy with the execution of the auction. If you take the time to shoot an attractive and well-composed photo of your item, it sends a message to the buyer that you're a conscientious seller as well.

A

The care you take in capturing a quality picture of your item may determine your success at auction.

Note: The more detailed your image is, the fewer questions your buyer will need to ask you, saving you time and helping to sell the item.

Figure A shows two shots of an item. In the first shot, the item was slapped down on the floor and photographed, with no thought given to lighting, background, or composition. The result is a passable image that doesn't show off the details of the item and doesn't make it look very appealing. In the second shot, the background has been simplified, the perspective changed to better showcase the object, and the lighting adjusted to reduce glare. The result is a much more attractive image that's bound to catch the eyes of a buyer or two.

Note: Since online auctions display images at a low resolution (72 dpi), you can get great shots from almost any digital camera, regardless of the size of the image sensor.

Selecting a background

The first thing to consider when getting ready to shoot is how you want to present your item. This starts with creating a simple background that shows off your item's assets. When selecting a background use these guidelines:

- Use a dark background for lighter or reflective objects.

- Select a gray or neutral background if you're shooting dark items, as white tends to create too much contrast in your image.

- Use common household items, like towels, pillowcases, or sheets as backdrops, but avoid anything with a distracting pattern.

- Avoid any material that's reflective, as it can add annoying highlights to your image.

Setting up the shot

Next, consider what you're going to use as your "stage." If you have an appropriate background, this can be almost anything from a tabletop to a professional light box. As shown in **Figure B**, we created a simple setup that uses a towel and a chair. This "stage" is portable, easily set up but not permanent, and gives us the flexibility to shoot the item from different angles.

Of course, this setup works best for smaller items. If you need to shoot larger objects, frame your shot so the background is uncluttered. Position the object against a wall or on a driveway so the area around it is consistent and doesn't divert attention from your subject.

Lighting the scene

Lighting is extremely important when capturing a quality image. Since most of us don't have professional studios in our houses, it's more than likely that we don't have professional lighting equipment hanging

around. Evaluate your potential light sources and create a setup that looks best with your item.

When setting up your lights, try to keep the levels even. Ambient room lighting is fine, as long as there's enough of it. Light coming from the side of the object usually provides better illumination, so avoid using bright overhead lights that can create unwanted highlights and shadows, as shown in **Figure C**. Move your lights around and observe how they affect the object. Try to position your lights to showcase the object's best features, evaluating your changes on the LCD panel of your camera as you make them.

Don't mix light sources such as incandescent and fluorescent, as it will send your image sensor into a tizzy. Even mixing natural and artificial light can cause color inaccuracies, so select one or the other. If you have a bright, cloudy day, consider moving your shoot outside, as these balanced lighting conditions can produce some of the best overall shots.

Once you've chosen a light source, set your camera's white balance for that type of light. This will ensure color accuracy and help the digital camera to select the best exposure settings.

Taking the pictures

With your scene and lighting set, you can start taking pictures. How you shoot the item is really dependent upon the dimensions of the object. Again, put yourself in the buyer's shoes. Think about which details are important to

B

Your setup doesn't have to be complex. Simple items like a towel draped over a chair produce perfectly acceptable results.

C

When shot with a harsh overhead light, our snow globe creates unwanted reflections that obscure image details. When the lighting is more even, the reflections diminish and all of the details are visible.

display. Choose an angle that gives the best representation of the size and shape of the object and fill the frame, minimizing the appearance of the background. If possible, take shots from many different angles and zoom in on small details that the buyer might find important. For example, if you're selling a piece of pottery, take a picture of the potter's mark on the bottom of the piece. Including significant details will leave fewer questions in your buyer's head and make him more likely to bid on your item.

If your item has any defects, scratches, or scrapes, make sure you take pictures of them, as shown in **Figure D**. Experienced auction buyers will appreciate your honesty, and the item will ultimately be easier to sell as the buyer knows exactly what to expect.

D

If your item is damaged, including a close-up shot will let the buyer know exactly what he's bidding on.

Note: *If your items are really small, such as coins, you might want to consider investing in a macro lens to magnify the scene and get more detail.*

Editing your pictures

Before we even get into enhancing your photos, a word of warning: While there are some aspects of your image that you can alter, make sure you aren't misrepresenting the item. Fixing scratches and scrapes or changing the color of your item in an image-editing program is out of the question and could get you into trouble. Image adjustments are fine, as long as they maintain an accurate representation of the product.

The first thing to do is crop any excess background from your image. As shown in **Figure E**, by removing the extra background around the item, it can now fill the frame and become the center of attention. Cropping can also help diminish a cluttered, distracting background.

Hopefully, you've captured a focused image, but if it's less than tack-sharp, consider sharpening the image a little. Be careful using sharpening, though. Add only enough to bring out the details, as too much sharpening can make the image look pixelated and noisy.

Finally, if your image looks a bit flat, perhaps due to poor lighting, adjust the brightness and contrast to balance out the scene. Don't mess around with color balance or saturation—if you provided appropriate lighting and set your white balance setting correctly, your colors should be pretty close to perfect.

Saving your image

The final step before adding your image to your auction site is to resize and save your image. Each auction site has different image size guidelines and rules, so check for a FAQ or Help section to get the correct dimensions and file size.

In general, most auction sites require an image that is 50 KB or smaller with dimensions less than 300 x 300 pixels. This size limitation is another reason why cropping is important. The smaller file size allows your prospective buyers to quickly see your image without having to wait for it to download. If you want to provide a larger image, consider adding a link so the buyer can choose if he wishes to view it.

Getting your file down to this size is usually dependent on how you optimize your image. For auctions, you'll want to use the JPEG file format, although you could get away with a quality GIF file. JPEG works best for continuous-tone images and will produce the most accurate colors. It also has several levels of compression choices when you save, so you can select a compression rate that's going to get your file size at or below the 50 KB target.

Posting your image on the site

Getting your image up on your site can be confusing, as each

E

In the first shot, it's unclear which item is for sale. Using cropping to eliminate excess image areas draws focus to the item and reduces file size.

auction site has different options and requirements. Some allow text only, requiring image files to be linked to an external site. Others offer image-hosting services for a fee, where your shots can appear on your auction page. When it comes time to add your images to your auction page, check the FAQ or Help section of your auction service. Since these sites want to make it as easy as possible for you to sell your items, they usually have straightforward instructions ready for you.

Creating a PDF slide show

Applications: Adobe Photoshop Elements 2, Adobe Acrobat® Reader®

While editing and capturing your digital images is fun, sharing them with others certainly offers the greatest reward. Slide shows on a computer screen are a great way to display your images, but these types of presentations often need to be run on your own computer using your own software. So, if you want to show off your images, you have to gather the family around your computer screen, an endeavor that might be as uncomfortable as it is impractical—or you have to email the slide show file, hoping your recipient has the right software to run the file.

What if you could create a slide show using a cross-platform file format that's easily emailed and runs on software almost everyone has already? You can do this by using Photoshop Elements to create PDF (Portable Document Format) slide shows.

The PDF file format runs on the Adobe Acrobat Reader application, which is installed on nearly every computer, and allows you to create simple slide shows with only a few clicks of your mouse.

Preparing your slide show files

If you can open the file in Elements, you can use it in a slide show. So, whether you use an image you found on the Web or one you captured with your five-megapixel digital camera, it can be included in the PDF. However, it's best to optimize your images to an appropriate resolution and size to reduce the total file size of your slide show. This feature does offer compression, but you're best off manually adjusting your images right in Elements.

Optimizing your files

The first thing you need to know is that the slide show displays full screen, which means low-resolution images from the Web could look pixelated when displayed. The images we want to display have a range of resolutions, so we're going to adjust them to a uniform 800 x 600 pixels at 72 dpi. To do this:

1. Open the image in Elements and select Image ▸ Resize ▸ Image Size and enter *800* in the Width text box and *600* in the Height text box in the Pixel Dimensions panel.

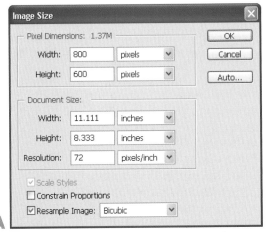

A
You can use Photoshop Elements' Image Size dialog box to format your images to a more appropriate file size for an onscreen slide show.

2. Deselect the Constrain Proportions check box and change the Resolution to *72* pixels/inch, as shown in **Figure A**, and click OK. Now, you have a more efficient and appropriate image file for screen display.

Note: *If you're creating a slide show with a large number of images, you may want to consider going to 640 x 480 pixels at 72 dpi, but we don't recommend going much lower than that. If you have a low-resolution image, such as one you downloaded from the Web, leave it at its original resolution to get the best possible image during presentation.*

3. Continue preparing images, leaving each one open in Elements as you go.

Creating the slide show

Once you've formatted your images, you can start building your slide show.

1. Select File ▸ Automation Tools ▸ PDF Slideshow and the PDF Slideshow dialog box displays.

2. Select the Add Open Files check box at the top of the dialog box to use your open files. When you're done, you'll have a list of filenames similar to those shown in **Figure B**. Because you left the image files open the software used those images to create the slide show. Not only does this save time over saving your slide show images into a separate folder, but you also don't have to recompress the

B

You can add images by first opening them in Elements and then selecting the Add Open Files check box or by using the Browse button to locate your files.

images, which allows you to better maintain the colors and details of your images.

3. You can remove an image from the list by selecting it and clicking the Remove button, or change the order of images by clicking on the filename and dragging it to its new location. Since it's hard to tell what an image is by a numeric filename, you might want to write down your image order before you open the PDF Slideshow dialog box.

4. Make selections in the Slide Show Options section of the dialog box, as desired. Here, you can designate how long each image remains onscreen before it advances, whether the images automatically advance, and if the slide show loops or stops at the last

image. You can also select from over a dozen transition effects, as shown in **Figure C**.

5. Click the Advanced button to bring up the PDF Options dialog box. As shown in

C

Elements offers 18 different transition effects you can use with your slide show.

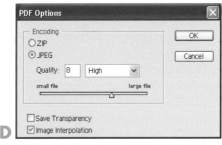

D

The PDF Options dialog box helps you set a balance between file size and image quality.

Figure D, this dialog box allows you to select either ZIP or JPEG compression and to set the compression level for the JPEG option. We recommend using the Image Interpolation option, which helps your image look its best onscreen.

6. Click OK when you're done setting your PDF options.

7. Click the Choose button in the Output File section and give your slide show a name and a saving location.

8. Click Save and then OK in the PDF Slideshow dialog box to finish the job. The software configures the slide show and gives you a message when the process is complete.

9. Locate your saved file and double-click on it to view your slide show. Acrobat Reader launches and displays your slide show full screen, displaying new images according to the interval you set.

Note: *In the unlikely event that you don't have Acrobat installed on your system, you can download the application for free from* www .adobe.com/products/acrobat /readstep2.html.

Part 4—Turning Your Digital Images Into Tangible Pictures

While digital photographs are an end product themselves, there are times when you'll want to print physical photographs from your images. There are many options for taking your photos from digital files to tangible pictures. In this part, we'll discuss how to prepare your photos for printing, offer suggestions for selecting photo paper, and take a look at different printer types and photo printing options.

Choosing the right resolution

Applications: Adobe Photoshop 7/CS, Adobe Photoshop Elements 2

Ah yes, the never-ending quest for finding a way to make a one-dimensional digital or print image look just as good as the three-dimensional item we saw with our own eyes. Is that so unreasonable? If we said the answer was yes, many of us would be out of a job. Therefore, we deny all improbability and continue to persevere.

Great strides have been made in technology, enabling us to inch closer and closer to our goal—with Photoshop being a key player. Regardless of how advanced technology becomes, though, the quality of the end product is still ultimately dependent on us. It's the decisions we make for capturing an object, digitizing it, editing it,

and outputting it that determine just how close we get to the real thing.

Every step of the way

There are fewer steps for preparing an image that will remain digital than there are for one that will be printed, but regardless of how an image will be viewed, one step we can't skip is specifying its size and resolution. Preferably, these attributes should be determined properly at the scanning or capturing stage, but that isn't always the case.

First things first

To edit the size and resolution of an image after the fact, we need to visit the Image Size dialog box in Photoshop and Elements, which displays the pixel dimensions of an image, as well as its physical dimensions and resolution. It also lets us change these attributes through resampling or scaling methods. That's a whole lot of terms, so let's begin with a brief explanation of *pixels, resolution,* and *resample.*

Pixels

Pixels are the unit of measurement a monitor outputs. A pixel represents one dot of information about the image. We typically refer to pixels in 1-inch increments, hence the term *pixels per inch,* or ppi. This isn't to be confused

200%

50%

A

This image has been scaled 200 percent larger than the original.

with *dots per inch*, or dpi, which refers to the resolution of an output device (laser printer, imagesetter, etc.) or input device (scanner, digital camera, etc.).

Resolution

The *resolution* of an image refers to the clarity or amount of detail shown on a monitor or printed page. Resolution is measured by either the dpi a PostScript device has placed on a page or the ppi a monitor is displaying. The resolution an image requires depends on its original size, reproduction size, and output method.

Resample

When we change the size and resolution of an image, we can choose whether pixel data is *resampled*—an automated process that involves sampling color from neighboring pixels, and then either removing pixels deemed unnecessary or adding pixels deemed necessary to preserve image quality.

Imagine that in print

If we place an image with a 300 ppi resolution into a page-layout application (such as Adobe® InDesign®) and then scale it down 50 percent, the result is an image with an *effective resolution* of 600 dpi. Likewise, a 300 ppi image scaled 200 percent larger renders an image

with an effective resolution of 150 dpi. The results of these actions are shown in **Figure A**.

Resizing an image this way not only affects its resolution, but also slows down the printing process. Cropping an image in a page-layout application isn't a solution either. It unnecessarily adds to the document's file size and also slows printing because the full image, although partially hidden, remains in the document. An image intended for onscreen viewing suffers a similar fate if resized or cropped outside of Photoshop.

PPI

Aside from color management, displaying and printing images is all about resolution. The resolution of an image should never be higher or lower than what the intended output device requires. Anything more is a waste and anything less produces poor results.

For example, look at the text shown in **Figure B**. Because it's been rasterized (flattened to reduce file size), it's now line art and has become resolution dependent. From left to right, the resolution settings for each letter are 100 dpi, 300 dpi, 600 dpi, and 1200 dpi. The letter on the far left didn't have enough resolution for the device it was printed on, resulting in a blurry image—whereas the second letter looks okay, but the edges

100 dpi   **300 dpi**   **600 dpi**   **1200 dpi**

B

The resolution of an image should be selected with the requirements of the intended output device in mind.

appear a bit jagged. The third letter, printed at 600 dpi, looks great since this is the proper resolution for the output device. The fourth letter doesn't look any better than the third even though the resolution is twice as high, demonstrating our point that when the resolution is higher than what the output device requires, it's just a waste.

LPI

So, how do we know if an image's resolution is too low or too high? It depends on the intended output device. The density of dots on a halftone screen is measured in *lines per inch*, or lpi—the number of lines of halftone dots printed per inch on a page. The lpi of an output device determines the necessary resolution.

LPI x 2 = DPI

The line screen or maximum resolution a desktop device can output is found in the Print dialog box, after selecting the appropriate driver. When outsourcing the job, ask the service bureau representative for the lpi. At the same time, ask what ratio is used to figure resolution; a 2:1 ratio is most common.

Yes, even in the design world, we can't escape math. However, this is fairly simple stuff. A 2:1 ratio simply means if the intended output device has a 150 lpi capacity, the images it outputs should have a resolution of 300 dpi (150 x 2). A 1.5:1 (150 x 1.5) ratio is also acceptable but anything more or less generally isn't, as shown in **Figure C**.

To put this in working terms: The average desktop printer has a line screen of 300 lpi (300 dpi). Therefore, if we intend to only print to a desktop printer, our images need only have a resolution of 150 ppi to print at a 2:1 ratio. Most full-color magazines are printed on a device that has a 150-line screen, so the images within it require a resolution of 300 ppi; line art being the exception. As we saw in **Figure B**, line art requires a higher resolution—at

TIP: If math really isn't your thing, let Photoshop do the brainwork. Simply click the Auto button in the Image Size dialog box to open the Auto Resolution dialog box (not available in Elements). Then, enter the line screen of the intended output device and select an image quality. *Draft* is the same as the lpi, *Good* means retain detail (lpi x 1.5), and *Best* means make smooth (lpi x 2). Click OK and the necessary ppi value for an image to print at the lpi you specified is calculated and entered in the Resolution text box.

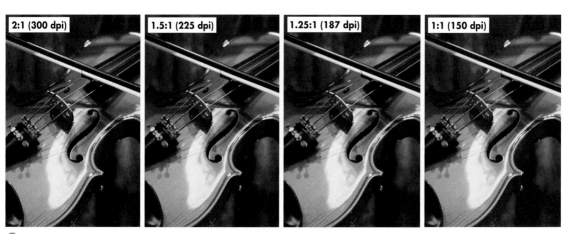

2:1 (300 dpi) **1.5:1 (225 dpi)** **1.25:1 (187 dpi)** **1:1 (150 dpi)**

C *It's important to know the maximum resolution a desktop output device can handle.*

least 300 ppi when printed on a desktop printer and at least 600 ppi when printed on an offset press. Table A shows lpi settings typically used to output various print materials and the recommended ppi settings.

Editing size and resolution

To maintain resolution and quality, images should always be edited in an image-editing program, such as Photoshop. More specifically, in Photoshop, an image's size and resolution should always be edited in the Image Size dialog box. For an up close and personal view of the Image Size dialog box, as shown in Figure D:

1. Open an image file in Photoshop or Elements.

2. Choose Image ‣ Image Size (Image ‣ Resize ‣ Image Size in Elements).

To resample or scale, that is the question

The biggest decision we have to make when changing size and resolution is whether we do so by scaling or resampling the image. When the Resample Image check box is selected in the Image Size dialog box and we decrease the size or resolution of an image, it's called *sampling down*. Pixels deemed superfluous are removed to accommodate the new size and/or resolution, and to prevent the image from becoming muddied with too much detail. Sampling down usually maintains image quality reasonably well.

Increasing the resolution of an image, however, is more

Table A: *lpi settings and their corresponding ppi settings*

lpi	General use	ppi for smooth	ppi for sharp
85	Newspaper ads	170	128
100	Newspaper editorial	200	150
133	Magazines and brochures	266	200
150	High-end magazines and brochures	300	225
175	Annual reports and high-end brochures	350	263

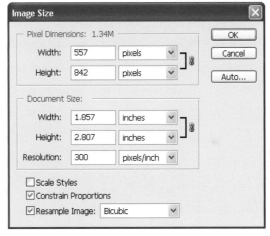

D

You can edit an image's size and resolution in the Image Size dialog box.

difficult. We can't magically add detail that never existed, so when an image is *sampled up*, new pixels based on the color of neighboring pixels are added to accommodate the increased resolution. Unfortunately, the result of this is typically less than favorable for the image's quality, not to mention the file size, which increases due to the added pixel data.

In Photoshop 7 and Elements, the dropdown menu to the right of the Resample Image option lists three methods: Bicubic, Nearest Neighbor, and Bilinear. *Bicubic* interpolation is probably the best choice because the equation that's used to sample pixels is the most accurate. The *Nearest Neighbor* option is faster but sloppy. The *Bilinear* option is okay but not as accurate in averaging the color of the surrounding pixels as the Bicubic method.

Note: *In Photoshop CS, you have two additional options. Bicubic Smoother is designed for better handling when enlarging the size of images, while Bicubic Sharper was created to help maintain detail when reducing the size of images. For most applications, the standard Bicubic option is going to do the job just fine, but you may want to give these other options a try.*

Pixel dimensions

The first section in the Image Size dialog box is Pixel Dimensions, which is followed by a number. This number more closely represents how much memory Photoshop and Elements require for us to work on the image and not the true file size.

The true size of an image file is important to know because it affects many things, such as printing and loading time. But the main purpose of the Pixel Dimensions section is to display the width and height of the image in either pixels or a percentage, and is one of two places where we can change an image's size in the Image Size dialog box.

By default, an image's width and height are displayed in the Pixel Dimensions section in, what else, pixels. Alternatively, you can choose Percent from the Width and Height dropdown menus to display the image's dimensions as a percentage. Sometimes it's easier to resize an image in these terms because you may not know the exact pixel dimensions you need an image to be, but you may know the image needs to be a certain percentage of its current size to fit in the space allotted for it in a publication.

To resize an image in the Pixel Dimensions section, the Resample Image check box must be selected, which it is by default. That means our only choices here are to resample the image up or down; scaling isn't an option.

To downsample an image, follow these steps:

1. Using the Percent option, enter a number less than 100 percent in the Width text box. If the Constrain Proportions check box is selected, a proportional number is automatically entered in the Height text box. It's a good idea to select this option to prevent resizing an image disproportionately.

TIP: In most Photoshop and Elements dialog boxes, pressing the [Alt] key ([option] key on the Mac) changes the Cancel button to the Reset button.

Table B: *Monitor sizes and their display capacities*

Monitor size	Maximum display (pixel dimensions)	Image size @ 72 dpi (document size in inches)
13-inch	640 x 480	8.89 x 6.67
15-inch	832 x 624	11.56 x 8.67
21-inch	1152 x 870	16 x 12.08

2. Or, you could directly enter new pixel values in the Pixel Dimensions section, and the image's file size updates, while the previous size displays in parentheses.

3. Click OK and the image scales to the specified percentage of its original size. Keep in mind, though, that this hasn't increased the resolution of the image. We've down-sampled the image; therefore, we've removed pixel data to reduce the size of the image and prevent unnecessary muddying.

Document size

This brings us to the Document Size section of the Image Size dialog box and the second place we can resize an image, edit its resolution, or both. The measurement system used to display the width, height, and resolution in this section is determined by the Units settings in the Units & Rulers area of the Preferences dialog box.

To change the resolution or size of an image without adding or subtracting pixel data, otherwise known as *scaling*, we can deselect the Resample Image check box. If we lower the resolution, the physical dimensions increase. Likewise, if we increase the resolution, the physical dimensions decrease. If we click OK after entering a new size or resolution, it appears as though nothing has happened because the pixel dimensions haven't changed. However, the size and resolution have indeed changed, as would be evident in print.

Scaling is a good method to use to turn very large, low-resolution images into small, high-resolution images or vice versa. However, if we want to resize an image without changing the resolution, we need to turn the Resample Image option back on.

On the Web, size still matters

Unfortunately, you can't prepare an image for online viewing and then turn around and use the same image with the same size and resolution, print it, and get the same results. In fact, one of the most common mistakes is to take images off the Internet and try to increase their size and resolution enough for print. It typically can't be done—at least not without some outside help from third-party plug-in software.

The standard resolution for multimedia is 72 ppi, which is based on the capacity of most monitors. However, the pixel dimensions of digital images can vary. **Table B** shows the most popular monitor sizes and their total display capacity.

When preparing images for online viewing, we need to create files that are as low in resolution and as small in file size as possible to ensure that pages load quickly. A 4-x-5-inch image with a 300 ppi can easily have a 5 MB file size, but if we change the resolution to 72 ppi and compress it we can get the file size down to 10 K, which is an acceptable file size for an image viewed online.

Why does 300 dpi look so good?

If human vision were equated to digital camera resolution, our ocular image sensors would weigh in at about 355 dpi. The part of the eye called the *fovea* is packed with cones that capture most of the detail and color sensitivity for our vision. This portion can distinguish seven line pairs per millimeter, or 355.6 dpi. We aren't going to go too far into the science of vision, but you get the point. Early digital cameras and high-end photo printers used to target 360 dpi, but manufacturers have come to settle on a resolution of 300 dpi.

Planning your prints to save photo paper

Applications: Adobe Photoshop 7/CS, Adobe Photoshop Elements 2

One of the drawbacks of digital imaging is the high cost of printing. While photo inkjet printer prices have fallen and quality has greatly increased, the price of consumables, such as ink and photo paper, remains high. It's easier than ever to download and print your images, sometimes even without using a computer. You can pop your memory card in a standalone printer, select your image, and print away. However, the ease of printing often leads to wasteful habits. Have you ever printed out a 4-x-5-inch image on an 8.5-x-11-inch piece of paper? There's a lot of space left on that page for other prints. We'll show you how to get the most from each page of photo paper.

Getting started

The first step when planning out a print job is to evaluate the sizes of prints you need to make. As shown in **Figure A**, our frame has eight openings for pictures. With a ruler, we measured each opening and made a list of the sizes needed. You can see that one of our openings is circular. If you run across a circle, oval, or any other odd shape, just measure the width and the height at their widest points. In this case, printing a circle isn't going to save us any room on the page, so we'll just make the image into a square.

Selecting the photos

Now, find the pictures you want to print and assign them to spots in the photo frame. Add filenames to your spots as you go so you can find them easily later. Consider the orientation of the print and use it to your advantage. For example, our circle opening is perfect for a close-up of a face, so we found one we liked and made a note of it.

Setting up your Photoshop file

The key to saving photo paper is to maximize the print area on your page. To do this, we'll use Photoshop (or Elements) to set up a document that represents the maximum print area for our inkjet photo printer. Then, we'll configure our photos to fit within these dimensions, leaving as little wasted space as possible.

A

This frame has eight openings of various sizes that we need to fill.

To maximize the print area of your page follow these steps:

1. Open Photoshop or Elements and select File ▸ New to create a new page. Our photo printer prints to a maximum page size of 8.5 x 11 inches, but there are models out there that can print at larger sizes.

2. Adjust the page size accordingly, if you're lucky enough to have a printer capable of printing larger sizes.

3. Enter dimensions for the Width and Height values in the New dialog box and then select the resolution target for your printer. For example, our printer leaves about a ¼-inch border around the edges of our image, which means we have an active print area of 8 inches by 10.5 inches.

4. Increase the dpi setting to match the resolution of your printer.

5. Make sure that the Color Mode is set for RGB Color, which is the color space used for digital cameras, as shown in **Figure B**.

6. Click OK to exit the New dialog box.

Note: *Does it matter which background you choose from the Background Contents dropdown list (the Contents panel in Photoshop 7 and Elements) in the New dialog box? Not really, but we prefer a transparent background, as it shows the edges of lighter images better. If you prefer a white background, it won't make any difference when it comes time to print.*

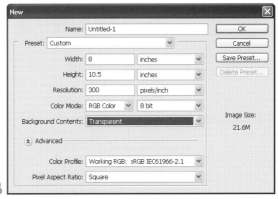

By determining the maximum print size of your printer, you can create a Photoshop document to take advantage of the entire print area.

Prepping your images

Once you have your print area defined, you can start adding pictures to the blank document. To do so, follow these steps:

1. Get out your list of frame dimensions; in Photoshop, open an image file you've chosen for one of the larger frame openings.

2. Examine the image. Are there areas you can crop out?

3. Consider how the shot is going to fit in the frame and what you want the main subject to be.

4. Use the Crop tool ⬚ to remove any excess image, if necessary.

5. Check the contrast, sharpness, saturation, color balance, etc.—make any adjustments you see fit. Now is the best time to make any image adjustments, as it gets more difficult to evaluate your images once you group them together in a layered file.

6. Flatten the image (Layer ▸ Flatten Image) before moving

on to the next step if you make any adjustment layers.

Resizing your shots

With your image cropped and adjusted, you can resize it to match the dimension of the frame opening. Our first image will go in the upper-left corner of the frame, an opening that measures $4^5/_8$ inches by $6^5/_8$ inches. Since we don't want any white space to show through the opening, we'll add $^1/_8$ inch to all sides, for a total addition of $^1/_4$ inch each to the height and width.

Once you've determined your image dimensions, use the following steps to resize the image:

1. Select Image ▸ Image Size (Image ▸ Resize ▸ Image Size in Elements) and note the Resolution setting, as shown in **Figure C**. For our file, the resolution is at 72 dpi, but the width and height are 28.444 by 21.333. We want to match our target file resolution of 300 dpi, but we don't want to have to upsample the image.

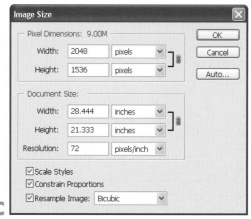

C

The dimensions of this image file are much too large, so we'll need to resize it to fit the frame opening.

Upsample means to increase the resolution of our image to match our master page's resolution. If we copied and pasted a file with a smaller resolution into our master page, Photoshop wouldn't change the resolution. Instead, it would reduce the size of the image to compensate for the higher resolution. For this technique, we need precise sizes, so continue with the next step to check whether your image has enough resolution to make it a viable choice.

2. Check that the Resample Image check box isn't selected in the Image Size dialog box. If it is, deselect it. Now the width, height, and resolution are linked together proportionally.

3. Enter *300* in the Resolution text box and note that the width and height decrease—in our case, to 6.827 by 5.12. Is this size bigger than your frame opening? If so, you have enough resolution with which to work.

4. Select the Resample Image check box and select Bicubic in the dropdown menu. Then, enter the target size of your frame opening, and click OK.

5. If the resolution is less than 300 dpi, you may want to reconsider your image choice or undo any cropping you might have done to create some extra resizing room. Of course, if you don't have these options and you're okay with a slightly

blurry image, go ahead and upsample the image to 300 dpi. Consider adding a little sharpening to the image to bring out the softened edges.

Transferring the image

Once your image is perfectly sized and at the target resolution, you're ready to transfer the image. To do so:

1. Select your image by choosing Select ▸ All from the menu bar or by pressing [Ctrl]A (⌘A on the Mac).

2. Select Edit ▸ Copy or press [Ctrl]C (⌘C on the Mac), and then click on the blank page you created previously.

3. Select View ▸ Fit On Screen so you can see your entire workspace.

4. Paste the image into this document by selecting Edit ▸ Paste or pressing [Ctrl]V (⌘V on the Mac).

5. Open the Layers palette by selecting Window ▸ Layers and note that your image has been placed on Layer 1.

6. Rename the layer with a more descriptive name by right-clicking ([control]-clicking on the Mac) on the layer name and selecting Layer Properties. If you're using Elements, simply double-click on the layer to open the same dialog box.

7. Enter a new name in the Layer Properties dialog box, and then click OK. You don't have to rename your files, but doing so makes them easier

to locate when you start adding more layers, as shown in **Figure D**.

We started with one of the larger images for a reason; since it's going to take up the largest area, it's most important to find space for it. Once we have our larger images taken care of, it's pretty easy to fill the blank spots with the smaller images.

Adding more images

For the next step, you'll have to rely on your spatial judgment when you check your dimensions list and select images to fill the blank spots. Repeat the previous steps for adjusting and resizing each image, and then copy and paste them into the master page. Each image is pasted into its own layer, so it's easy to work with each one individually. When arranging your images, it's a good idea to leave a little white space between to make them easier to trim out.

To fit the images on your page, you may need to rotate some of the photos. There are a few ways to do this, but here are the two most common methods.

To rotate the content of a layer individually using a menu command, use one of these methods:

- **Photoshop:** Click on your target layer in the Layers palette, and then select Edit ▸ Transform. As shown in **Figure E** on the next page, another menu opens with a variety of transform options. Most likely, you'll be rotating your image 90 degrees one direction or the other, but you

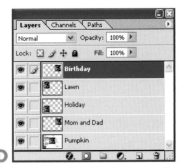

D

You can give your layers descriptive names to make your images easier to locate.

can choose whichever option gets the job done.

Note: *You can't transform a Background layer. If you need to rotate the contents on your Background layer, select it and then choose Layer ▸ New ▸ Layer From Background. Now you can rotate the layer as much as you want.*

- **Elements:** Click on your target layer in the Layers palette, and then select Image ▸ Rotate. Next, select an option from the menu that meets your needs.

- **Photoshop/Elements:** Alternately, select the target layer (anything but a Background layer), and then press [Ctrl]T (⌘T on the Mac).

A bounding box appears around the boundaries of your image. If you place your cursor on any of the corners of the box, you can rotate the image freely when you click and drag in the direction of the rotation. If you want to limit the rotation to 15-degree increments, hold down [Shift] as you drag. This makes it easier to get a 45- or 90-degree rotation.

Printing and saving your file

Depending on the size of your frame, you may not be able to fit all of your pictures on one 8.5-x-11-inch sheet. That's okay; the main goal is to maximize the space usage on each sheet you print. For our large frame, we needed to make a new page to accommodate the remaining images, so we simply started the process over.

It's a good idea to save your master page as you work. Not only will it be helpful if you have an unfortunate computer crash, but it also allows you to print out shots for admirers of your frame. If someone mentions he likes a particular photo, you can easily pull up the master page and print him a copy.

Since we took the time to properly set up our document, printing the page should be a breeze. Just remember to give the print proper time to dry before you handle it or place the images in the frame. If the print is still wet, you can get fingerprints on the page or the print could stick to the glass in the frame. An hour or so should do the trick.

Fill in the blanks

The only thing left to do is cut out your images and fill in your frame. Use a small piece of tape to tack the prints down as you go; this helps keep them in place while you arrange all of the prints. Our filled frame is shown in **Figure F**. It only took two pieces of photo paper to print out all of our images. Plus, our prints fit into their places perfectly and have enough overlap to cover any small shifts in positioning. With the high cost of printing supplies, being smart about the use of your resources gives you more opportunity to create great prints without wasting a lot of money.

E

The Transform option menu makes it easy to select how your image is rotated.

F

With some simple print planning, you can save money by using your photo paper wisely.

Selecting photo-quality inkjet paper

You've spent months researching and picking out the perfect digital camera and inkjet photo printer. You've taken stunning pictures, painstakingly edited them on your computer, and sent them to print, expecting museum-quality prints to grace the walls of your home. However, your colors look like a puddle of mud, your fine details have disappeared, and ink has soaked through the paper. What happened? Well, most likely you put ordinary office paper in your inkjet printer. Creating high-quality inkjet prints requires high-quality inkjet paper, specially designed to keep colors bright and details sharp.

Getting started

The best place to start when choosing photo paper is the manufacturer of your printer. Almost every printer producer has a set of inks and paper that corresponds with the make of your printer. This combination has been scientifically configured to produce the best quality images using that particular printer. However, while some people think you should always go with the manufacturer, this isn't necessarily the case. Trying the photo paper produced by the printer manufacturer is a great place to start, but stopping there could cause you to miss out on some good options. Printed image quality is highly subjective, so the paper designed for your printer might be too white or not glossy enough for your taste. Give the paper designed for your printer a try and use it as a benchmark when you experiment with other papers.

So many options ...

Next, we'll go over the qualities you should look for when selecting an inkjet paper. Some of these qualities might be more important to you than others, but understanding their importance will help you choose the best paper for your printing needs. Consider the following qualities:

- **Paper thickness.** A good photo paper should feel heavy in your hands, but not stiff. If a paper is too thick, the printer may have trouble feeding it across the ink jets. If the paper is too thin, it not only tears more easily, but its low opacity allows light to pass through, skewing your colors. Papers that have a good thickness are usually made with denser fibers, which absorb and hold ink more accurately. They also tend to bleed and spread less, as the ink is readily absorbed into the paper. Plus, a thicker paper mimics the feel of traditional photo paper, giving it a better perceived quality.

- **Whiteness.** The whiteness of a paper directly affects the brightness and saturation of your colors and the sharpness of your details. Consider the situation we described previously—typical office paper has a brightness number in the 80s. Typical inkjet paper is usually slightly brighter with numbers in the 90s. Quality photo paper usually has a brightness number in the high 90s to over 100. Can a paper be too bright? Sure, but in most cases, brighter is better. However, a paper that's too bright might overwhelm softer colors or delicate shading, so avoid the extremely bright papers if your image has these attributes.

- **Paper finish.** One of the most subjective attributes of photo paper is the texture of its surface. Some prefer glossy; others prefer matte. While the finish of your paper is really a matter of preference, there are a few things to consider. Glossy papers display bright colors better than matte paper, but can be easily marred by smudges and fingerprints. Matte paper is more resistant to damage and works well with images that have large areas of color. However, matte paper can cause shadow details and darker colors to look muddy.

But photo inkjet papers don't just start and stop with glossy and matte paper. Now you can choose from semi-gloss, satin, luster, high-gloss, photorag, watercolor, semi-matte, mirror gloss, pearl, and many others. Follow your preference and experiment with different types of papers to find which finish works best for you.

Note: *Keep in mind that if your print is going to be framed, having the highest gloss paper isn't going to make a difference and might actually cause unwanted reflections on the paper surface.*

- **Archival ability.** One of the challenges inkjet paper manufacturers are working on is the longevity of the paper. Currently, most photo papers last only a few years before a degradation of image quality begins to occur. However, advances in paper technology and archival inks are extending the life of photo inkjet prints into decades. Look for a photo paper that can resist the effects of the sun, has some level of water-resistance, and has been designed to maintain color accuracy over a long period of time. Also, keep in mind that archival papers and inks tend to require a longer drying time, so it may not be the best choice if you're working in a production environment where time is of the essence.

Setting the scene

Once you've decided which qualities best embody your perfect photo inkjet paper and you've selected the perfect substrate upon which your prints will reside, make sure that the paper is compatible with your printer. Most manufacturers offer extensive lists of printer and ink compatibility, so check to see if your printer is on the list. Also, check the documentation to find the best settings for your printer, even if you're using paper made by the same manufacturer of your printer.

Choice is good

The print is the last link in the imaging chain. So, why wouldn't you take the time to select the photo paper that's going to make your images look their best? By knowing your options and making decisions based on your personal preferences, you can find the one that's right for you.

Using an inkjet printer

With the advent of cheap inkjet printers, everyone suddenly had the capability of cheaply printing his own color images. While this was practical and cost effective, the images were far from archival. Most of the prints would only last a few years at best, and as a result, weren't appropriate for any pictures you wanted to last a long time, such as fine art prints (giclée) or even family photos like our baby picture shown in **Figure A**.

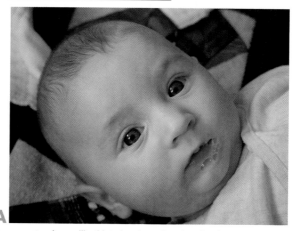

A

If you want an image like this to last, it needs to be printed on archival stock.

Now things have changed. Many inkjet paper/ink combinations have the potential to outlast traditional color prints. The expansive growth of the inkjet market has led to a diverse array of inks and papers that give you a variety of imaging possibilities as well as improved image permanence.

Inkjets for the masses

Inkjet printing has become wildly popular and with good reason. Printing color images in the traditional color darkroom is expensive and hard to maintain. Because of this, most photographers have other companies print their images for them. With the inkjet and programs like Adobe Photoshop, photographers and artists have the opportunity to print their own digital work at lower costs, whether they're printing giclée or commercial work.

Epson dominates the inkjet market and makes a wide variety of printers and papers for both professionals and consumers. However, only a few of their consumer-level printers are capable of producing archival images with Epson archival inks. Many ink manufacturers have leapt in to fill the gap for those photographers who want image permanence as well as high quality.

Ink sets

In the inkjet arena, there are basically three types of ink. You can get pigment, dye, or a hybrid of the two inks. For serious image stability, you need to use inks with as much pigment in them as possible.

Companies such as ConeTech, MIS Associates, and Lyson are making archival color ink sets that are compatible with many Epson printers. All these companies say their ink is best, but you can find out the longevity data on these third-party inks as well as Epson's from an independent test lab called the Wilhelm Research Institute. Their results are made public on their Web site (www.wilhelm-research.com) and most of the ink companies will tell you how they were rated by them as well.

Monochromatic beauty

If you prefer the beauty of black and white or platinum prints to color, you can also get archival monochrome ink sets for your inkjet printer. Monochrome ink sets are sold as quadtones because they contain three gray inks and a black. These produce really rich tones and, when combined with art papers, can give you wonderfully textured and long-lasting images like our image in **Figure B**.

Ink on paper

Ink isn't the only important factor for creating long-lasting images. The quality of the paper is just as important for maintaining image permanence. Archival paper has been around for a long time, but companies have only recently started experimenting with coatings to enhance ink take up and

longevity. The high demand for different substrates has led to a plethora of papers in different colors and textures. Each one takes ink a little differently, so you need to know which papers work with which ink sets. This requires experimentation as well as research.

Dedicated quality

Experimentation can be frustrating as well as expensive, for many users. To alleviate these types of problems, Epson produces totally dedicated systems. If you use their archival papers and/or archival inks on their specific printers, then you eliminate a lot of variables in the process. This means you can get down to the business of making great prints quickly, but you're more limited in your media choices.

Color management

Color management is a major problem when working with many different inks and papers. To do any type of accurate printing, some amount of color

management needs to take place. This means acquiring ICC profiles for the papers you want to use. With so many different inks and papers, this becomes difficult and expensive, as most profiles aren't free. Such Web sites as **www.inkjetmall.com** can provide you with profiles for a variety of papers and inks for a price.

Better color for less hassle

If you want even fewer printing hassles, Epson has been working to streamline the image to print process with the development of Print Image Management, or PIM. Basically, this is a protocol that creates a profile of your images based on settings you make in your camera. When this image is printed on a PIM-enabled printer, instructions on how to print the image are passed on along with the image data. Epson has licensed the PIM technology and many of the digital cameras released recently are PIM-enabled, which gives you the opportunity to make reasonably long-lasting prints with less hassle.

Images that last

When you need your images to last more than two or three years, it's important to get the right materials. Many factors contribute to image degradation, including light, ozone, air contaminants, and humidity. Once you have an archival print, you still need to take care of it properly for it to last and that almost always means covered or under glass!

B

Archival inks will keep this baby picture around until long after the baby grows up.

Online picture services

Applications: Adobe Photoshop 7/CS, Adobe Photoshop Elements 2

Digital image printing used to be an expensive service that was only provided by a relatively small number of businesses. However, with the advent of digital minilabs that can print on standard photographic papers, digital photofinishers are popping up everywhere. With the Internet, location is no longer much of an issue. You can upload your files to a variety of companies without ever leaving your home, making online photo finishing an attractive option.

Online caveats

Like everything on the Internet, your enjoyment of these sites may be somewhat limited by your connection speed. People with faster connections have an easier time uploading lots of images, while those with slower connections may find the upload time frustrating. Another factor is the speed of the company's servers. Some of the servers we uploaded to were very slow, but this changed depending on the time of day we uploaded.

Another thing to keep in mind is that, in the past, users of certain online photo sites have lost their images in the site's demise. It's important to keep your own archive of images on your computer, so you don't get burned in a sudden dotcom collapse.

Preparing your images

Digital devices, such as monitors and scanners, function in the RGB color space. The new digital photo minilabs fall in this realm as well. Within the spectrum of the RGB color space, there's the *sRGB* space, which is a device-independent description of color that helps different devices exchange information about color accurately even though the individual devices differ slightly in their interpretation of color.

Since the sRGB color space is independent, it can be described and attached to an image through the means of a profile. When you prepare your images for print at any of these companies, you'll get the best results by attaching an sRGB profile to the image to ensure better translation of color data from your computer to the minilab printer.

Of course, you'll get the best results by working in a color-managed environment, such as Photoshop or Elements, with a calibrated monitor. Unfortunately, the sRGB profile doesn't ensure perfect pictures because of the vagaries of chemistry development and how well these companies maintain control in their minilabs.

Printer and paper

Another factor you want to consider when choosing a lab is the paper they use. The most archival of all silver halide papers used for color photographic prints is Fuji's Crystal Archive, which has a rating of 60 years when stored under appropriate conditions. Other common papers, such as Kodak's DuraLife, Agfa, and Konica papers have significantly shorter life spans. There's quite a lot of debate about appropriate testing methods to determine archival quality and how to take proper care of a print. The predicted life span for any paper assumes that the print is stored under glass, out of direct sunlight or in an album. Pictures that are lying around or improperly stored degrade faster.

However, longevity isn't everything. Each of the paper types has slightly different color characteristics. You may find that you prefer a matte surface or the color rendition of Kodak papers over Agfa, or vice versa. Most of the photo processing companies are using Fuji Crystal Archive or Kodak's Edge 8 paper.

Making the decision

When selecting an online photo processor, you can often receive free prints. This allows you to try their service, for a small out-of-pocket cost.

Your decision may be further refined by choosing the company that prints on the paper you like or offers options that you find the most interesting. Even if you don't want to use a company consistently, you may find that some of their products make them worth using on occasion. These companies also offer regular film processing and scanning services.

Getting the most out of your desktop printer

Having a document professionally printed can be a costly endeavor that many small businesses and individuals simply can't afford. That doesn't mean there aren't other options available. More and more people have opted for printing small order business cards, brochures, and marketing materials in-house. With the plethora of desktop printers currently on the market, there's a model suited for everyone. Putting some extra thought into the process of picking out your desktop model, and then taking the time to get to know your printer, will reap long-term benefits.

One dot at a time

Primarily, the three most popular types of printers used in the home and small office are inkjet, laser, and solid ink printers. Although the ink source is different, they all print using fine dots to create halftone patterns, which produce the illusion of tone and/or color, as shown in **Figure A**.

Inkjet printers

Inkjets originally made their mark as a low-cost alternative to color printing. While the initial cost of a printer is low, the ink cartridges can get costly, especially if you need to replace them frequently. By the time you've purchased a few ink cartridges, you could very well have purchased another printer. While the refill kits are

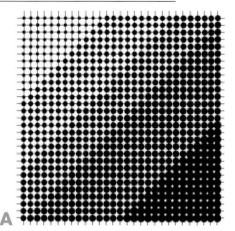

A

The arrangement of dots in a halftone grid creates the illusion of a tonal gradation.

a cost-saving alternative, they may produce such undesirable results as clogging the print heads and streaking your pages. Inkjet printers are generally best suited for low-volume printing needs. They're a good choice for color composites, photos, and other low-volume color prints. Most use four colors of ink—cyan, magenta, yellow, and black—but you can also purchase six-color inkjets that additionally have light cyan and light magenta. The colors from these printers are more vibrant.

There are a few downfalls to inkjets. First, because the ink is wet, heavy coverage on standard-weight paper creates ripples. Inkjets prefer inkjet-specific paper, which can be more costly. Also, even though they aren't as slow as they used to be, they're still slower than their laser counterparts. And finally, if you purchase a high-end inkjet expecting to use it for color comps, there's a chance you'll also have to purchase a RIP (Raster Image Processor) to go with it, which can cost thousands of dollars.

Laser printers

Laser printers have come down in price in recent years, to the point where even a color laser is affordable. Lasers are exceptionally well suited for printing crisp text. They're great for quick printing of high volumes of text or graphics pages. Many of them come with multiple paper trays and some hold paper up to 13 x 19 inches.

One downfall to laser printers is that the toner coverage doesn't always remain consistent. As the toner gets lower, your coverage may become lighter than when the toner was brand-new.

Solid ink printers

Solid ink printers use solid sticks of wax-based ink. The wax is melted and then sprayed on the drum, which is then picked up by the paper. They produce results similar to that of a dye-sublimation printer, yet still print with dots. Because of the type of ink they use, the color is always consistent. The ink sticks themselves are handy because each color is shaped differently, making them foolproof and easy to install. They print faster than most color lasers, since they don't have to rotate toner cartridges around a carousel. Their price is competitive with color laser printers. One downfall is that the printed materials don't laminate well,

since a laminator will reheat and spread the ink around.

Note: *Dye-sublimation printers are the best for producing photo-quality prints and they're becoming much more popular. You'll find more information on dye-sublimation printers in the next article.*

Selecting your photo printer

There are many options to consider when evaluating photo printers. It's important to keep your printing style in mind when starting out. Do you like to print large prints? Is it important to you to print borderless prints? Let's take a look at some of the features to evaluate when comparing different printer models:

- **Cost.** The starting place for any purchase is determining your price range. When looking at photo printers, there are actually two prices to consider: the cost of the printer and the cost to keep it running. While the printer may be a bargain, the cost of the ink and paper can quickly add up. When doing your research on printer prices, check out the replacement cost of these consumables and factor them into your decision.

- **Print size.** As mentioned earlier, some photo printers can print larger than the standard 8.5 x 11 inches. However, printing smaller than this size might be more desirable, as photo paper is now available in many conventional sizes, such as 3 x 5 inches and 4 x 6 inches. Check the range of print sizes for the printer—by printing at the size you want you can avoid wasting expensive photo paper.

- **Speed.** You might ask yourself: What do I care if it takes a few extra moments to print out a picture? Well, these moments can add up when printing high-resolution photo prints. Anxiously watching a print crawl out of the printer is no fun, so take a look at the print speed. Ignore information based on printing text documents and focus on the image-printing speed.

- **Connectivity.** Most photo printers offer either USB or serial connections, but some dye-sublimation printers require FireWire or SCSI connections. Check out the available connections on your computer before purchasing a printer—there's nothing worse than having to install a SCSI card before you can print.

  There are a few photo printers that don't need a computer at all. You just plug in your memory card, select your print, and your print comes out. If this sounds good to you, make sure that the printer accepts your memory and look for a model with a small LCD panel for reviewing your images before you print.

- **Longevity.** As mentioned earlier, dye-sublimation prints

last longer than inkjet prints. If you still want to go with an inkjet print, look at the print permanence data for the printer. Some manufacturers offer special inks and papers for creating longer-lasting prints, so do your research if this is important to you.

- **Resolution.** This may seem like one of the most important features to look for, but most inkjet photo printers offer a resolution that produces great prints. Plus, more resolution isn't always a good thing, as too many drops of dye can make your colors look muddy. Certainly be aware of the resolution of the printer, but use print quality and color accuracy as the ultimate measurements.

Setting up your document

There are some things to keep in mind as you work that will increase the aesthetics of your final piece. There are more things to consider when preparing a document to send off to a print vendor than when printing from your desktop printer. Nonetheless, some steps need to be taken to ensure accurate printing to your desktop printer.

Resolution

Most imagesetters and commercial printers print at about 150 line screen, which requires your images to be supplied at 300 dpi. This follows the general rule of thumb that your scanned resolution should be between 1.5 and 2 times the line screen. An average desktop printer doesn't have the capabilities of producing a line screen that high; therefore, it doesn't require a resolution that high. Typically, the size of your scanned images doesn't need to be much higher than 150 spi (samples per inch) for an average quality laser printer or inkjet, and between 240 and 300 spi for a high-resolution laser or photo-quality inkjet printer.

Working with line art is a bit different. A good rule of thumb when working with line art is to scan your image at the resolution of your output device, up to 1200 spi. So, if you'll be printing from a 600 dpi laser printer, then 600 spi is the setting you should use to scan your line art. But if you're printing from a 1400 dpi photo-quality inkjet, 1200 should be your limit. A few examples are shown in Table A.

Borders and bleeds

Most desktop models can't print closer than ¼ inch to the edge of the page, thus creating a natural border around your page. You should experiment with your printer and find out what its natural margins are, as they differ from printer to printer. If you want your document to have a full bleed, you'll have to print on larger paper, and then trim it down. Some of the high-end color laser printers come with paper trays that support up to 13-x-19-inch paper, allowing users to print an 11-x-17-inch document with crop marks, so it can be trimmed down to have a full bleed. If you're printing a large volume this way, it might be beneficial to do your printing, and then pay a nominal fee for an office copy place to do the trim work for you. Doing this manually can be a time-consuming process, and it isn't always entirely accurate.

Not your ordinary paper

Printing from your desktop printer doesn't mean you have to stick with plain white laser paper. Visit a local paper supply store and see what your options are. Usually, they'll supply samples of the papers they have

Table A: *Scanning settings for common desktop printers*

Printer type	Recommended samples per inch for scanning continuous tone images	Recommended samples per inch for scanning line art images
Desktop laser–600 dpi	100–150 spi	600 spi
Desktop inkjet–600 dpi	100–150 spi	600 spi
High-resolution laser–1200 dpi	150–300 spi	1200 spi
Photo-quality inkjet–1400 dpi	150–300 spi	1200 spi

for purchase. Take a printout of your piece with you to match up with a few samples that you think would complement your piece. There are many different varieties of paper to choose from, varying in color, texture, and weight. Just make sure that whichever paper you choose is suitable for printing on your particular printer.

As we mentioned earlier, many people opt to print their business cards and other materials in-house, partly because printer qualities have improved over the years, and partly because the pre-perforated stock is so easy to come by. Avery® makes a line of products that includes labels, business cards, greeting cards, and other miscellaneous pre-perforated card stock. Each box comes with a template that you can either scan or measure and set up your document accordingly. A helpful way to control waste is to photocopy this sheet, then when it's time to print, do a couple of test-runs on the page you copied to make sure your page items align correctly.

Know thy printer

In today's world of plug-and-play, we seldom take the time to read the manuals and other materials that come packaged with our printers and other peripherals. This is a bad habit to get into. Often there are useful warnings and precautions outlined in the manuals, which can save you time and money in the long run. Get to know all of your printer's features. Almost all laser printers have an LCD screen right on the printer with a menu button and options to scroll through. These options take you through different features, such as paper handling, error logs, printing configuration pages, and more, depending on your printer.

Updating drivers

Visit your printer manufacturer's Web site to gather as much information as you can. Every so often, check for printer driver updates, which are available for download. These updates usually fix problems that have surfaced since the last release. Go to the support areas of the Web site, and check for known issues and printing problems other people are having. You may find a simple fix to your problem and avoid the need to hire a technician.

Downloading fonts

Many printers store fonts, or more specifically, outlines of fonts in their memory. These are known as *soft fonts*. Sometimes they're only stored until your printer is turned off, so make sure to check your manual for specifics. Some of the higher-end laser printers come with their own hard drive and memory. You can upgrade the RAM on your printer just as you can with your computer. The more memory your printer has, the more fonts you can download to it.

Usually a printer includes a utility in the installation software, which enables you to manage your printer's fonts. Having the fonts stored on the printer saves time when spooling your documents, because the printer already has the necessary fonts loaded into memory. Many printers download both PostScript and TrueType fonts, but check the manual that came with your printer to be sure.

Calibrating your printer

You can calibrate many printers just like you can calibrate scanners and monitors. Some high-end color laser printers include color calibration utilities built into the printer software. Among the menu items, there's typically an option to print out a test calibration page that customarily includes color and gray samples, which you'll have to visually inspect for accuracy. Then, by using the available options, you can manually adjust the amount of cyan, yellow, magenta, and black until you've achieved your desired results. If your printer doesn't include a type of color calibration utility, then simply calibrate your monitor to match your printer's output. If you're going to be printing primarily from your in-house desktop printer, then you only have to calibrate for your internal system.

Purchasing consumables

Consumables are the extras necessary to keep a printer up and running. They include toner cartridges, ink cartridges, drum kits, fuser kits, maintenance trays, and others, depending on the type of printer you use. The cost of the consumables is calculated into the cost-per-page price. The cost of an ink jet cartridge is low compared to a laser toner cartridge, but it won't last as long. Checking out which types of consumables a printer has before you purchase it will give you a good indication of what kind of maintenance to expect on it.

Duplexing

A nice feature to have is the option to have a printer automatically duplex your document. A duplexing unit prints one side of the page and then reverses the paper to print the other side. Some printers allow for manual duplexing in which you feed the paper through by hand for a second printing on the reverse side. Make sure your printer has this feature before you do that, though, because otherwise you risk having the toner smear and smudge. More importantly, you risk actually damaging parts of your printer, so make sure to check the manual for any information regarding duplexing.

Dye-sublimation printers

Some digital photographers use an inkjet printer to put their images down on paper so they can see their printed pictures as soon as possible. Others upload their digital files to an online photo finisher to get the durability of photo paper. Both options yield high-quality images, but what if you could get the immediacy of an inkjet and the durability of a photo print combined with smooth, rich prints? Your solution is a dye-sublimation (dye-sub) printer, a technology that has been used for digital printing for many years. However, these models were geared toward professional photographers who needed a reliable way to produce high-quality, high-volume images (think pictures with Santa), and they came with a professional price tag for both the hardware and the consumables. We think it's time to take a closer look at this printing technology, since the price of dye-sub printers is falling, and this technology is becoming more attractive to digital photographers of all skill levels.

How the dye-sub process works

Instead of using ink droplets, a dye-sub printer uses a transfer ribbon to print images. The ribbon is really a plastic film that contains patches of cyan, magenta, and yellow dye, and a layer of protective material. To make a full-color print, the paper must make four passes through the printer to apply these four layers. When a print is made, the paper passes under a heating element that causes the dye on the ribbon to vaporize precisely to correspond to the density needed in the print. As the paper passes under the heating element, the vaporized dye diffuses onto the surface of the paper. The paper then retracts into the printer to repeat the process and receive the other two color layers and the final protective layer. After the fourth pass, you're left with a print that can be immediately handled (no drying required).

Note: *The protective coating guards the print from handling damage, such as fingerprints and moisture, but also from light damage caused by ultraviolet rays.*

Pros and cons of dye-sub printers

As dye-sub prints are made from a continuous piece of film, they're considered continuous tone images and look the most like a traditional print. The dithering essential for inkjet printers to replicate images is nowhere to be found in dye-sub prints, so color and contrast transitions are smooth. Let's take a look at other ways dye-sub stacks up to inkjet printers.

Resolution

Most dye-sub printers print at 300 dpi, but because the process is so different it's hard to say how this equates to the higher resolutions of inkjet printers. If you like extremely sharp prints, a photo inkjet printer does a better job, as the smooth transitions found in dye-sub prints produce softer images. However, since dye-sub prints look so much like "real" prints, they're often preferred to the graininess of inkjet prints.

Paper size

Inkjet printers have the edge when it comes to paper size. Most dye-sub printers are configured for a fixed paper size, usually 4 x 6 or 8 x 10. This means your choices for paper size are very limited, where inkjet prints can usually print a range of sizes. Dye-sub printers are for photo printing only, where inkjets can be used for a range of printing tasks. Inkjets can also print on a range of paper types, while dye-sub choices are usually only matte or glossy photo paper. Of course, there are options for dye-sub printers like photo stickers, but don't expect to print a photo on a 100 percent cotton envelope as you could with most inkjet printers.

Speed

Print speed varies from one printer to another, but overall, dye-sub printers print faster than inkjet printers. Even though the paper must make four

passes through the printer, these passes are very quick. Plus, you don't have to wait for the ink to dry before you handle the print.

Cost

Dye-sub printers are more expensive than inkjet printers, but keep in mind that the inkjet printer manufacturers are really more interested in selling you ink refills than the printer. As new dye-sub models become available, their price should become more competitive. As far as consumables, the price of a dye-sub print is slightly more than an inkjet print. Dye-sub printers use special cartridges that contain a fixed number of prints and paper that is designed for each printer, so you pretty much have to stick with the media made for your printer.

Size

Because dye-sub printers don't need the space for several ink cartridges and the assembly to move them back and forth, they can be made much smaller. In fact, some dye-sub printers are barely bigger than the paper size they print on. Many models are easily portable with battery support and media slots for printing right from a memory card. Some even have built-in LCDs for previewing your image before you print. More advanced models even have some limited image-editing software built in.

Working with low-resolution images

Perhaps you mistakenly saved over your original high-resolution file with a low-resolution version. Or, you received an image optimized for email or one downloaded from a Web site. Maybe you set your digital camera for a low-resolution setting to pack more images on your memory card. In any case, you've got a low-resolution image file that you want to print with high-resolution results. While turning a low-resolution image into a high-quality print isn't always easy (or possible), there are a series of steps you can take to evaluate your image and make adjustments to produce the best possible print.

Be wise when you resize

The first thing that comes to mind when presented with a low-resolution image for printing is to resize it to a higher resolution. This technique is called *resampling*, as your image-editing application literally samples the image data and re-creates that information at the new resolution. When pushed to its limits, resampling can pixelate the image, soften contrasts and transitions, and wash out colors. However, sensible resampling can produce acceptable results.

The key to resizing an image without decreasing its quality is to be conservative. You can only push an image so far before it starts to look bad, so you might not be able to turn a 72 dpi image into the 300 dpi resolution used by most photo inkjet printers. Instead, try to get as close as possible without affecting image quality. Start with a modest resample and view your image onscreen at 100 percent to get a good idea of how it will print. Examine your image for excessive pixelation and a soft, fuzzy look that can come from excessive resampling. If it's distracting onscreen, it's even more evident on paper, so undo your resize and try resampling to a lesser resolution.

At this point, you may very well have an image that looks good enough to print. If you're satisfied with your results, feel free to print the image and skip the next steps. As we mentioned, resampling is the beginning of the process, but you can move on to printing whenever you're satisfied with your results.

Make your adjustments

After resampling your low-resolution image, the next step is to make any image adjustments that can improve picture quality. The human brain has a remarkable ability to fill in the blanks when there isn't enough detail, but it's hard to trick it when you have poor color balance and contrast. If you can't squeeze more resolution from an image, concentrate on making image adjustments to improve what you have. Images that have been resampled almost always need some sort of sharpening to improve contrasts and edge details, but be careful when applying this feature.

When you resample, the image can get slightly pixelated, and over-sharpening is only going to make this more obvious, as shown in **Figure A**. Other options include adjusting the brightness and contrast in your image, boosting saturation to compensate for any washed-out colors, using Adobe Photoshop's Levels command to better define the tonal range of the image, and applying a slight blur filter to the image to hide any pixelation.

Apply special effects

If your image is still plagued with poor color balance and pixelation, consider using special effects to cover up these problems. Most image-editing applications have dozens of options to choose from, so take a look at which ones are available to you and select one that fits the content and purpose of your image. A common approach is to apply a watercolor effect, which softens the pixels and colors to effectively hide most quality issues, as we have in **Figure B**. If your image is suffering from poor colors but has good contrast, consider converting the image to black and white. If your image has good colors but bad contrast, perhaps a rough pastels effect would produce a good result. As we mentioned, there are lots of cool effects out there, so when your low-resolution image needs a little help, experiment with them to create some memorable images.

Working with printer settings

Your last line of defense is your inkjet printer. Since every inkjet printer has different options and capabilities, you'll have to do some searching for what settings might improve the

Original

Acceptable

Too much

A

Sharpening can do more harm than good, so be careful when applying it or your image could look pixelated.

quality of your low-resolution image. However, here are a few things to look for when exploring your inkjet printer settings. Always select the highest possible quality setting or the highest resolution available. Most printers allow you to speed up a print by sacrificing quality, but for our purposes we don't mind waiting for the print if it means improved quality. If you have the ability to control the size of your ink droplets, select the finest possible setting to help give the illusion of more detail in your image. Finally, look for any type of enhancement mode, such as Epson's PhotoEnhance options. These allow you to define the content of your image and let the software make printer settings to optimize output.

We took our most pixelated version of our canine friend and applied the Watercolor filter in Adobe Photoshop to produce an acceptable high-resolution image.

When you get to the print stage, there isn't much you can do, but by taking advantage of whatever features are available, you may be able to create something good.

Inkjet T-shirt transfers

Application: Adobe Photoshop Elements 2 or any image-editing application

Do you remember going to the T-shirt transfer store and picking out your design from a wall of choices, usually some sort of glittery rainbow or the logo for a heavy metal band? Your image would be sandwiched into a large heat press and immortalized on the ¾-sleeve T-shirt of your choice, at least until it started to flake off in the washing machine. Since the technology behind this haute couture was merely a really hot iron, the designs were what brought people into the store. With the proliferation of inkjet printers for home use, paper manufacturers have created inkjet transfer papers that can be printed with a custom design. So, whether you're creating T-shirts for a local fundraiser or just putting a picture of your puppy on your shirt, we'll tell you how to turn your images into wearable art, as we did in **Figure A**.

Shirt details

When selecting an inkjet transfer paper, it's important to know what kind and color T-shirt you'll be applying it to. There are basically two versions of paper: one designed for use with light-color fabrics and one for dark. The version for dark colors has a special backing that blocks the fabric color from showing through the transfer. Remember that inkjet printers don't print white, so any white or light-colored areas in your design are going to allow the color of the fabric to show through. Technically, either version will work on any color, but get the right type so your colors turn out as you intended. Also, check the manufacturer's specification on which fabrics can be used—usually any fabric will do as long as it's made up of at least 50 percent cotton.

Prepping your image

There are many applications that can be used to create your custom design, but try to use one that's geared toward image editing so you can easily adjust colors and resolutions. Some image-editing applications come with commands for creating inkjet transfers, or you can search the Web for free utilities to help you design and print T-shirt transfers. Many paper manufacturers have free software applications you

A

With today's inkjet transfer papers, it's easy to put your images on all types of media, including T-shirts.

can download, so check your packaging for availability.

Keep the ink flow low

The key to a good transfer is printing the right amount of ink on the transfer paper. Too much ink can make a mess when it comes time to apply the transfer. A setting of 360 dpi is recommended for most papers, but you can get away with less if necessary.

Create your design

There really aren't limitations when it comes to creating your design. You can incorporate text, combine multiple images, apply special effects, or anything else you can do in an image-editing application. Just keep in mind that your medium (fabric) isn't going to show detail as well as your computer screen, so keep your text big and bold and avoid subtle details that are likely to get lost in the transfer process.

Give it a flip

Since you'll be placing the finished piece facedown on your T-shirt to make the transfer, you'll need to flip the image so it comes out in the correct orientation. If not, your design will be backward when you make the transfer. This isn't always noticeable with images, but you'll notice it pretty quickly if you have text in your design. You can do this in your printer software, but we suggest doing it in an image-editing application. Then you know the image has the correct orientation before you print and you won't have to wait anxiously to see if your

B

For the best-looking transfer, trim off any extra material before you use the iron.

printer flipped the image correctly. Each application uses slightly different commands to flip an image, so figure out how to flip it horizontally. For example, Photoshop Elements for Windows uses Image ▸ Rotate ▸ Flip Horizontal.

Printing your design

It's a good idea to print a test sheet on regular paper before you print on the much more expensive transfer paper. That way you can check the size and placement of your image before you make a costly mistake. When you're ready to make the final print, load a single sheet of paper into your printer tray, making sure you're printing on the right side. Most transfer papers have a grid pre-printed on the wrong side to help you out.

Go ahead and print, but don't plan on making the transfer until the print is completely dry, usually about a half hour or so. Then, use scissors to trim off the excess transfer paper, leaving no more than 1/8" around the edges, as shown in **Figure B**.

Leaving excess transfer material can cause unsightly patches of cloudy-looking transfer material on your shirt.

Applying the transfer

To transfer the design to your T-shirt, follow the manufacturer's instructions exactly. The process may differ slightly, but most recommend a very hot iron and a flat, hard surface (an ironing board is too soft). Once applied, let your transfer cool for a few minutes and carefully peel away the backing paper to reveal your new fashion statement, as shown in **Figure C**.

Post-transfer care

Your new shirt is ready to wear, but wait a few days to wash it so the transfer can fully adhere to the fabric. Some types require a quick vinegar bath to help the adhesion process, but check the instructions that came with your transfer paper for specific information. Turn your shirt inside out when washing to get a little more protection and reduce any abrasion caused by other items in the wash. Then, dry your shirt at a normal setting, but keep it inside out for the same reason. You may wish to hand wash and line dry if you want to be extra careful.

Note: *If your design starts to fade, some manufacturers suggest placing a piece of the removed backing paper over the design and reapplying the iron for a few seconds. We didn't test this claim, so check with the manufacturer of your transfer paper to see if you have this option.*

C

Allow your transfer to cool completely before you peel off the backing paper.

Glossary

Amplified noise: Noise that occurs in the blue channel of an image. The human eye is less sensitive to blue light, so the blue channel must be amplified to make it equal to the red and green channels, and by nature this results in a nosier blue channel. Usually only visible when viewing the blue channel directly.

Aperture: Opening that allows light to pass through a camera lens. Apertures are usually expressed in f-stops—smaller f-stops represent larger apertures. A larger aperture lets more light hit the camera's CCD— approximately twice as much light for each full f-stop increase.

Aperture priority: Camera mode that allows you to set the aperture manually while the camera adjusts the shutter speed automatically to arrive at a correct exposure. Usually used to limit or expand depth of field.

Aspect ratio: Ratio of the width to the height of an image. For example, the aspect ratio of an image measuring 6 x 4 can be listed as 3:2 or 1.5:1.

Automatic matrix metering: Metering based on an algorithm composed of configurations of different lighting situations. Useful in outdoor photography or with backlit subjects.

Available light: Light from the natural environment, not light the photographer has introduced with lamps or flashes.

Balance: Relationship between your main subject and the other elements in the image, such as background, props, surroundings, and other subject matter.

Bit: Smallest unit of data a computer uses to store information.

Bit depth: Number of bits used to describe color information in an image. Higher bit depth results in more colors and larger file size.

Bitmap: Another term for a digital image.

Bloom: Condition that occurs when oversaturated pixels spill overflow onto adjoining pixels. Can occur whenever you shoot in bright sunlight or use a flash.

Bracketing: Taking several shots of the same scene at different exposures, thus reducing the chance that you'll miss a shot due to under- or overexposure.

Buffer memory: Memory that stores image data before it's processed and saved to storage media.

Burst mode: Mode where your camera takes several shots rapidly to record a series of images. Allows you to take sequential shots or multiple shots of the same scene. Also called continuous, sequential, and multi-shot.

Burst rate: Number of images a digital camera can take before the buffer memory is full.

CCD (charge coupled device): Device used to sense images and record digital photographs. Composed of multiple electronic sensors that convert light to electrical charges.

CMOS (complementary metal oxide semiconductors): Electronic sensor that converts light to electrical charges. Offers better resolution and uses less energy than charge coupled device (CCD) sensors.

CMYK: Primary colors (cyan, magenta, yellow, and black) of an image as seen by reflected light.

Close Up mode: Produces photographs with images ranging from 1:10 ($^1/_{10}$ of life size) to 1:1 (life size).

Color depth: Number of bits assigned to each pixel in an image and number of colors that can be created from those bits.

DOF (depth of field): Distance between the closest and farthest objects in focus. A wider aperture, such as f/2, produces a shallower depth of field, and a smaller aperture, such as f/11, produces a wider depth of field.

dpi (dots per inch): Used to measure the detail of a print. Also refers to the resolution of an output device or input device.

Dark pixels: Bright spots in an image resulting from thermal noise.

Digital zoom: Magnifies the image you're photographing in a manner similar to what an image-editing application does. Results in a lower-quality image.

Downsample: Decreasing the size or resolution of an image.

Exposure: Amount of light reaching the camera's image sensor. Determined by aperture and shutter speed settings.

Exposure compensation: Feature that allows you to increase or decrease your camera's sensitivity to light, which results in a lightened or darkened image.

fps (frames per second): Designates number of frames captured per second in a particular mode.

f-stop: Number expressing the focal length of the lens divided by the aperture of the lens opening. Used to determine the amount of light that will hit the camera's sensor.

Fill flash: Flash designed to fill shadows and backlit subjects.

Focal length: Distance between a lens surface and the camera's image sensor. The larger the distance, the stronger the magnification factor of the lens. Measured in millimeters, focal length determines the angle of view for your camera. A camera with a short focal length has a wide angle of view, while a camera with a long focal length has a narrower field of view.

Full bleed: Image area that extends to or beyond the trim edge of a print.

Giclée: High-resolution fine-art inkjet prints.

Grayscale: Range from black to white, including shades of gray.

Hot shoe: Mount used to attach external flash or slave units to a camera. External flashes usually have longer range and better battery life than the internal flash unit.

Image resolution: Spatial resolution or the number of pixels in an image.

ISO settings: Standards created by the International Organization of Standardization that measures a sensor's sensitivity to light.

JPEG: Image saved in a compressed file format created by the Joint Photographic Experts Group. Best format for displaying images on the Web.

lpi: Lines per inch. Measurement of the density of dots printed per inch on a page.

Line screen: Printing term to describe the halftone screen frequency of a print.

Lossy compression: File compression that changes some of the color values in an image to save disk space. The greater the compression, the more visible the pixel color changes appear; with low amounts, the compression is almost unnoticeable.

Lossless compression: File compression that reduces file size without changing color values and degrading the image.

Macro lens: Lens that helps you to photograph extremely close subject matter with sharper focus and less distortion.

Macro mode: Produces photographs with images ranging from 1:1 (life size) to 80:1 (80 times life size). Also known as photomicrography.

Noise: Any type of digital disturbance that reduces the clarity of the signal received by a digital camera. Results in odd colors and spots in random areas of an image.

Overexposure: Photograph that turns out brighter (washed-out colors) than the photographer intended.

Oversaturated: Condition that occurs when a pixel takes on more charge than it can store. Oversaturated pixels often spill their overflow into adjoining pixels and thus create bloom.

Pixels: Unit of measurement a monitor outputs. A pixel represents one dot of information about the image. Typically referred to in 1-inch increments, hence the term pixels per inch, or ppi. The term is derived from "picture element."

Print resolution: Number of pixels in an image in one dimension (vertical or horizontal) divided by its printed size in that dimension. Print resolution is measured in pixels per inch, or ppi.

RGB: Primary colors (red, green, and blue) for transmitted light as used by monitors, slide projectors, etc.

Recycle time: Length of time it takes your camera to be ready to take the next shot or burst of shots.

Resampling: Automated process that involves sampling color from neighboring pixels and then either removing pixels deemed unnecessary or adding pixels deemed necessary to preserve image quality.

Resolution: Clarity or amount of detail shown on a monitor or printed page. Measured by the number of dots per inch (dpi) a PostScript device has placed on a page or the pixels per inch (ppi) a monitor is displaying.

SLR (single lens reflex): Camera that uses a single lens to both view and take pictures.

Shutter lag: Delay between the moment when you press the shutter button and the moment when the image is captured.

Shutter speed: Length of time the shutter is open to allow light to shine on the camera's sensor when taking a photograph. Expressed in fractions of a second, slower shutter speeds can produce blurred and undefined images, while faster shutter speeds (usually those at 1/250 or less) can also eliminate natural shakiness of a handheld camera, giving you sharper images.

Silhouette: Backlit subject that's darkened to the point where you can only discern the outline and no other details.

Slow synchronized (slow sync): Flash mode designed for poor lighting situations. Camera's shutter will automatically operate at slower speeds in this mode to capture the illumination behind the flash-lit subject.

Spot meter: Metering mode in which the camera measures only in the center of the frame.

Stuck pixels: Bright spots in an image resulting from thermal noise.

Telephoto lens: Lens that lets you enlarge the subject you're photographing at a higher magnification. A telephoto lens acts to help you "zoom in" closer, and is sometimes called a zoom lens.

Thermal noise: Noise produced as a result of the heat generated by the CCD over the course of long exposures. Causes bright spots, known as hot pixels or stuck pixels, to appear in images. Too much of this sort of noise can render an image practically unusable.

Underexposure: Condition that occurs when an image sensor can't get enough light to capture an accurate reading. Results in misinterpretation of the signal, noise production, and a darker image than the photographer originally intended.

Upsample: Increases the resolution of an image to match the master page's resolution. During this process, new pixels that are based on the color of neighboring pixels are added to accommodate the increased resolution.

White balance: Camera setting that allows you to designate the light source so the camera properly reproduces image colors accordingly.

Wide-angle lens: Lens that expands the field of view the camera can fit in the frame. A wide-angle lens actually acts to help you "zoom out" farther.

Index

Your trusted source for proven solutions to help boost your computer expertise

Element K Journals
A Unique Source of "How-to" Information

Element K Journals is the leading provider of computer technology journals and information products. If you want to become a more proficient computer user at work or in your personal pursuits, you'll find that Element K Journals is the best source for comprehensive, innovative, and timely information on the technology that is changing the world today.

For more than 20 years, Element K Journals has contributed to the professional growth of more than one million computer users through an extensive lineup of print and digital products, covering everything from business and graphic design applications to programming tools and languages to operating systems.

To make the most of the new opportunities technology presents, our customers depend on the high-quality information found in Element K Journals' products and services. You can expect information that's specific to your needs, and solutions that are immediate, proven, and practical—all provided by our responsive editorial staff who put their years of experience to work for you!

- More than 35 monthly "how-to" journals

- A family of productivity boosting CDs and computer-based training (CBT) products

- Handy quick reference cards

- Complete Quick Skills Kits

- Essential quick reference guides

- Searchable online archive

- Downloadable PDF reports

- FREE weekly email tips service

Unparalleled Resources
Our editors strive to provide you with insight into software applications that isn't available anywhere else.

Business Professionals Library
Microsoft® Access
Microsoft Excel
Microsoft FrontPage®
Microsoft Office
Microsoft Outlook®
Microsoft PowerPoint®
Microsoft Windows®
Microsoft Word
Corel® WordPerfect® Suite
The Internet

IT & Web Professionals Library
Microsoft Windows Server™ 2003
Microsoft Windows
Microsoft Visual Basic®
Microsoft Active Server Pages
Computer Support/Help Desk
Sun Solaris™
Macintosh®
Novell® NetWare®
Oracle®
Microsoft SQL Server™
Web Development

Graphic & Digital Designers Library
AutoCAD®
Creative Designer
Digital Photography
Adobe® Illustrator®
Adobe InDesign®
Adobe PageMaker®
Adobe Photoshop®
QuarkXPress™
Web Design

For more information, visit
www.elementkjournals.com.
Or call 1-800-223-8720.

Monthly Print Publications

Our expert editors provide you with the information you need to succeed, written in a concise and easy-to-read format that includes step-by-step instructions, solution- and task-based techniques, and more, all supported by detailed illustrations.

Searchable Online Archive

EKJ Online offers you unlimited online access to the current month's issue of the same journal you receive in print. Plus, a searchable database of all the articles published in that journal for the past few years is always at your fingertips. The intuitive, easy-to-use search capabilities of EKJ Online help you find the precise information you need—anytime, anywhere.

Quick Tips Compilations

Instantly increase your expertise with a variety of software applications and operating systems with these hot tips, cool tricks, and timesaving shortcuts. Choose from our Smart Tips and Quick Tricks booklets on more than 20 different topics or one of three searchable Smart Tips and Quick Tricks CD-ROMs with more than 400 tips each.

Quick Reference Cards

The step-by-step instructions and clear illustrations on each six-panel tri-fold card make software applications and operating systems easy to understand. Keep one next to your computer or tacked on the wall for quick, everyday use.

Productivity Boosting CDs

The hundreds of one-of-a-kind Microsoft PowerPoint background templates on these CDs will help you be more creative, save you time, and increase your productivity. Make every presentation spectacular using these CDs.

Article Compilations on CD

Element K Journals' Quick Answers CDs are convenient, fully searchable CDs filled with two years' worth of full-length articles from our monthly journals. You can search by keyword, topic, and article title to find hundreds of step-by-step articles and timesaving tips that will ensure you're working smarter, not harder.

Computer-based Training CDs

Learn new computer skills whenever it's convenient for you with QuickSkill® CBT CDs. The lessons on each CD are interactive simulations of the actual software, and even include an audio component that talks you through each step. Skill assessments at the end of each lesson provide you with immediate feedback on your level of understanding.

Downloadable PDF Reports

Get instant access to "how-to" information designed to increase your productivity. Our award-winning expert editors hand-picked more than 20 full-color pages of the best step-by-step, "how-to" articles from Element K Journals' monthly publications, covering your favorite solutions and techniques.

Digital Photography Skill-Building Series

This is an ideal resource for all digital camera users! Do you wish you could shoot like the pros, share your photos with others, and add special effects to your images? Learn how, quickly and easily, with our new *Digital Photography Skill-Building Series*. Six 20-page full-color guides give you tips and techniques for getting the most out of your digital camera.

FREE Tips

Sharpen your competitive edge with the tips, tricks, techniques, and expert advice you'll learn from Element K Journals' FREE Tips—delivered weekly to your email inbox. Sign up for the FREE Tips of your choice now at **www.elementkjournals.com/tips.asp**.